Guinea Pig in the Sky

by Refried Bean

Guinea Pig in the Sky
by Refried Bean

This book contains three collections:

A Whole Bunch of Stupid Poems

My Pet Died on Christmas

**Tripwatch Overlay:
A Book About Prayer**

Copyright 2016 by Refried Bean

Acknowledgements

Thanks to all my friends who have been there for me.

Thank you Wendy Mauritz, Claire Bateman, Catherine Polit, and Drena Fagen.

Thank you also to all the committees and task forces and code 5 responders.

Thanks especially to everyone at First Presbyterian Church in Greenville, SC, Grace Church, Woodruff Road Presbyterian Church, First Presbyterian Church in Columbia, SC, Fairforest Church in Greenville, Young Life, and YEF at NYU.

Thank you Food Network.

Thanks also to the Binders and Binders who NaNo.

A Whole Bunch of Stupid Poems

By Refried Bean

"Surely he took up our pain, and bore our suffering."
Isaiah 53:4

When I lose weight

When I lose weight
I am going to write a book called
Fat People Can Succeed
and people will say
hey you're not that fat
and I will say
yeah and I don't succeed.

Invention

What if there's another invention like the wheel
that's really obvious and really necessary
but we're all missing it somehow and haven't invented it yet?

Gusseppe and Delores had their baby.

Their third little peanut was born today
at the Cloisters museum and monestary.
So now Flippy and Zippy have a little brother named Dippy.
I am very happy for my imaginary pet angel mice
and thankful for all the other little mice that helped them.
I know all the other museum visitors here
who have spent the day
seeing the beautiful pictures of Christ and the unicorns
are also happy about the good news
and what can I do but pray a prayer for all of us
and ask God to help everyone be good at soccer.

poem

What if lightning is from God taking pictures of us?

Poem

Spaghetti with meatballs and cheese and sour cream.

It starts with the microwave and ends like a dream.

I like the yummy yummy things that help me have good days.

And poems like this are likely just a part of some odd phase.

Fudge

what if you made fudge so good that you decided to present it on judgment day as your life's work but what if you were supposed to instead say "Jesus dying on the cross' is what I present" but what if you were already trusting that so much that you went ahead and presented the fudge.

And the Emily Dickinson poems too

guys when I die
I will be a missionary to heaven
and I will tell them all about
the cool video games and soda that we have on earth.

haiku

toy machine
at the grocery store
almost empty

poem

people are going to think I am just darling
when they see my forgiveness.
i will walk by without cursing at people
and they will say that is so adorable.

poem

no one seems to want to say it
but I'll say it:
swans aren't that great.

I am the fourth guinea pig.

Over the lands of rolling thunder
with the horizon glimmering past the cages dawn,
Fred, Roger, and Dave eat their breakfast,
and I eat my ice cream cone,
free from the oppressive bars
that separate the burden and life,
free from the growing sentiments of discontent
and dwindling waters.
I am the fourth guinea pig who finds the day,
who shuffles around and drinks a coffee drink.
Who uses my freedom to check on the others.
I am the fourth guinea pig.

another poem

guys i can't seem to think of another poem idea today
so what about a poem called "I am the fifth guinea pig."

Let me tell you what I think about your little poems.

I think they're great.
I really do.
Me, I don't say stuff about how clowns hurt my grandfather
because I think it's not appropriate,
but it is your right to say that and more
and buy me an ice cream if you don't mind.
I like mango ice cream.
Also I'm thinking about converting to Catholicism.
That's not a joke and maybe all of a sudden
mentioning it in a poem
when really I am serious and it is a big life decision,
I mean some people might not think that is a good idea.
But nailing Jesus Christ to a cross wasn't a good idea either
and yet people did that and now it means I am forgiven,
according to the Protestants,
or it might be just one more thing
that I am symbolically also guilty of,
which is also what the Protestants told me,
so you can see why I am confused.
I think this is a breakthrough
that I witnessed myself.

Bonus Poem

On Judgement Day,
when God sifts through my poems and says
actually only one of these counts as a poem
and the other ones are really what we would call
"mild expressions" or
"profane offenses that jeopardized the future of humanity"
you know what
I wont let it get me down guys
I will say well I guess I am just a one poem poet
and it's a good thing that poem
was a prayer
asking God to give everyone
5 million dollars and a pet guinea pig
and a magic coke machine!!!!!!!!!!!!!!!!!!!!!!!!!!!!!!!!!!

Taking a Little Break

I'm not going to contact my therapist on her vacation
to let her know about the new guinea pig poem I wrote.
It was a good one, you know,
when I made that little joke about being the fourth guinea pig,
because what really does that mean?
Well do you know who would be able to tell us what it means?
My therapist. But she is on vacation and this is not an emergency.
If I called crying and then told her
that it was because I wrote a good poem
then she might be relieved,
but she might also need another vacation,
when really, we have the guinea pig poem that we needed.

poem

I can't just tell myself
to think of a poem
and then think of something.
But what I can do
is write down that I cant think of anything
and then not provide a link or reference
to the poets who could.

poem

What if in the future
people figure out how to not exist
and they do that for vacation

poem

I know I'm not the antichrist
because I do not have the leadership skills.

poem

Really your behavior might be totally normal
for someone with schizophrenia.

Sayings

Christianity is when God burns your sin instead of you.

It might not be that Christianity keeps a person from being a jerk
as much as it keeps them from being such a jerk.

Alarming

You know what would be ironic
is a smoke alarm starting a fire.

Guys I really did see a lizard shortly after asking God to let me see a lizard.

Dear God, may I please see a lizard on my vacation.
Please may I see one and no one else gets to see one.
Forgive me, God, please let everyone see a lizard.
Please make everyone's homes
be crawling with lizards so much
that people can't get stuff done or go to work.
Forgive me God, please just make there be
a reasonable amount of lizards.
Please make there be the amount of lizards that there already are.
God, I do not need to see a lizard to be happy.
Forgive me for baseing my happiness on seeing a lizard.
Forgive me God for making you regret the creation of lizards.
God please will you just keep the lizard situation
however it was meant to be
and if I was meant to see a lizard then I will see one
and if I was meant to write a poem about seeing a lizard
will you please help me know what to say
and please erase everyone else's poems.

Soft serve

At church camp, the lady told us that in life
we would have steak dinner friends and ice cream friends,
and the steak friends were the ones
who would really be there for you,
and the ice cream friends were just for fun.
But I remember that same lady was the one
who saw me in the bathroom later that week
with a whole ice cream cone stuffed in my mouth,
a little bit worried as I tried to finish swallowing it
after my friends dared me to eat it whole.
So I think that makes her an ice cream friend,
though she was there for me, and rare.

poem

If I ever give birth,
I hope it is a beagle.

poem

I feel so happy right now
but it could just be a seizure.

Just a little idea

They should make eye makeup
that is also medicine for pink eye and styes.

The shockwaves and the thunder and the cookies

my weekend was so glorious
that peoples faces are going to melt off
when i walk down the street to get coffee this morning.

the way i knew to buy some benedryl but not take it
and yeah i did call my friend who is a doctor
and didnt pay her but it was still glorious enough to shatter the
wooden frameworks of all the buildings in my neighborhood
though I guess the apartments are mostly brick

but anyway when i went to volunteer work
immediately after taking the guinea pigs and two cages to the vet
because it was so hot and i didn't have the life skills
to get air conditioning,
i mean there is glory in that
even though people kept tripping over me at volunteer work
because i was just standing around
wondering why there were no skittles at the food pantry

but skittles is what will be falling from the sky
and pelting everyone in their faces
as I walk humbly to the coffee shop
with the glimmering light shining all around me

and warming the streets
though that might also be from the 90 degree weather
that made me ruin my diet with 2 cartons of juice
and all the ice and soda that a person could ever drink
while doing nothing whatsoever for hours and hours
because I'm stuck on that level of a video game
that wont beat itself.

inspection

At the grocery store,
I suddenly decide to become an inspector
for America, or really of America,
to see how America is doing
and using the grocery store as the representative sample.
There seemed to be lots of food,
and some pots and pans,
and I found the orange Jello I was hoping for.
So I feel like I should go ahead and give America a good report,
though because of all of the other unnaccounted factors,
I think that the score of 3.99 that comes up on the receipt
seems about right and I am happy to sign off on it.

What happens when you run out of poem ideas?

Storms a brewin, Fifi.
That's what they told me at the coffee shop,
though they didn't call me Fifi,
which is okay with me.
And now that I think about it I could have said
Coffee's a brewin', Sallassandra,
even though that's not their name either.
But anyway I got a vanilla latte
and of course am very thankful
and am safe indoors
and ready for my next adventure
which is finishing this poem
with a legal statement
of my intention to sue every coffee shop in America
and every gas station
and every school and hospital
for all the times they have not told me
about either a storm about to happen
or about all the discounts at other coffee shops and gas stations.

One of the pizza poems ever written

Some people are getting a little sassy around here
and I think it's because they want ice cream
or because the air conditioner is loud
or because they applied for a job
or because it's pizza time it's pizza time.

Ok let's everyone calm down.

We can get a pizza.
Pizza pizza pizza pizza
This is not a joke everyone.
Hi Is this is the pizza place?
Do you have my credit card number on file? Why is that?
I don't understand why that is okay but I would really like a pizza.
Well which kind would I like.
Well I think you probably know that and more
if you have my credit card number.
Ok yes I do want cheese and bacon and pineapple.
Yeah I did okay on that school paper
but the teacher said my joke was rude.
Ok yes please deliver the pizza this time.
I am assuming that you have the key to my apartment.
Ok the pizza is in the oven.
What? It's in my oven?
Warming up because you guys already made it and brought it over?
Because you knew I would want pizza today
after taking the extra anxiety medicine?
Yeah it is true because the panic attacks came back
when my sister said not to give her kids cotton candy.
Oh I guess you knew about that.
Ok because there is a pizza place at the beach too.
Well I wish you guys would have helped yourself to a slice or two.
Oh you did? Ok and you got some limeade from the store.

Ok and some ice cream.
Ok well that is great then I will talk to y'all next week.
Oh yeah I do have that volunteer event Friday.
Ok so it will be a couple of weeks and yeah I would appreciate if you would bring back my pet guinea pigs that you let your kid bring to school for show and tell.

Cake poem

guys when I write a diet book
it is going to be called
"Done with Cake"
and it will be about how I am never eating cake again
except guess what.
I will eat cake a lot
because I love cake
and I'm not going to stop eating cake
just for a book title
and honestly I am thinking about
not writing the book at all
and letting this poem be enough for now
but what will never be enough is cake.

a break in the light
is a break in the fight
which is a break in the right

I feel that doing my laundry in a timely manner
will just make me seem like I am a person who gets chores done
and won't that make me a target for the forces of darkness?

Consolation

Mental Illness is rough sometimes
but I have found that I do really well
in Hibachi restaurants
where they give free dessert
to people who hit themselves.

poem

you know what
honestly
some people aren't that wretched.
They generally do what they are supposed to
and they even clean things some times like do dishes
and wear clean clothes and say nice things to people
but everyone makes mistakes
and people get into a little trouble or
maybe have some kind of chronic neurological problem
that makes them curse at people
and smell like dirty socks
but maybe that's why there are waterfalls in heaven
or maybe its not you know
maybe everything everyone does
is just so little kids can laugh
or maybe it all has to do with a jelly bean factory
or maybe potatoes are in the eye of the beholder.

Guys I am not going to give my air conditioner a name but I think we all know what its name would be don't we.

my air conditioner reminds me of jesus christ.
people say don't say that
but you don't know what the air conditioner did for me
people say you dont know what jesus christ did for you.
well that is exactly what i am saying
people will say jesus christ is not as loud as your air conditioner
and i will say oh really there will probably be a roar
when he comes back on the clouds
just like my air conditioner
but people might still say
jesus did not break the law
like your air conditioner bracket
that probably doesn't meet legal standards
and I will say you know what
you got me there everyone
I will say you got me there
I guess we won't be having church services in my apartment
I guess I will just sit back and drink a lemonade
and eat some fortune cookies that say
Your air conditioner has changed your life hasn't it
and you want to buy everyone an air conditioner
but you also want to keep your money for lemonade and cookies.

Tough choice

you know what
a tough choice is
for a funny kid
is to say hey when you grow up
do you want to be a comedian
or a roast beef sandwich?

Hurricane Warning

Guys what if the same hurricane came back years later to bother everyone?

A heartworming animal story

Ralph didn't see any great emails in his account but there was a survey from the pet store that he went to a couple days before to buy food for his pet guinea pigs. He started to fill it out like he did with all the surveys, giving the service people a ranking of the highest scores possible, which was what he would want people to do for him. He knew that was helpful because he had just finished working in a retail store before enrolling in the college classes he was currently taking. The survey asked if he had any specific examples to share about how he had been helped in the store, and as he had been doing more and more frequently on all the surveys he filled out, he made up a story about how his cashier had helped him. In fact, he said she had saved his life and his pets' lives in an emergency involving a falling aquarium display and an attack from an animal rights extremist group.

Three weeks later, Ralph got a letter summoning him to court. It seemed that Ralphette, the cashier who had helped him, was being charged with some kind of misdemeanor based on an incident with a different customer that same day.

When Ralph got to court, Ralphette, a wonderful and darling nice girl his same age, took the stand and described a situation where a yucky bad person tried to touch her on purpose when she was cashiering and told her she didn't know anything about pet food and then came around into the desk area to grab her shoulder and she had hit him and called him a kangaroo poacher and a french fried frog leg peddler.

"I would do it all again the same," she said.

The lawyers said they had checked all the paperwork and surveys from that day and found Ralph's survey suggesting that that very cashier had intervened in a hostage situation. They wanted to charge Ralph with fraud.

Ralph took the stand and answered some questions from the lawyers and then the judge, who seemed like a nice and reasonable person.

"Ralph, do you realize what it means that this survey became court evidence and you said that there was a hostage situation when there wasn't?" the lawyer said.

"Well honestly, to me, this court case is what seems like a hostage situation," said Ralph. "I doubt that Ralphette gets paid enough to deal with this kind of ongoing harrassment." Ralph was quiet and looked at Ralphette.

"Do you have anything else to say?" the judge asked Ralph.

"Yes," said Ralph. "I was wondering if you guys ever do marriages at this court."

"We do," said the judge, and she helped Ralph and Ralphette get married that afternoon. Ralph and Ralphette loved each other a lot and adopted several rescued greyhounds and built a whole wall of aquariums in their house.

.

Thought

What if the only good thing anyone had to say about your book
is that no one would be jealous and wish they had written it?

Another thought

A theology discussion I refuse to have
is the question of whether Jesus Christ
was an orange and not a human.

New Criticism

Hey everyone what if there was a type of literary theory
called schizophrenia literary criticism
where the main goal was to read the text
and figure out the meaning of all the secret messages
that are directed to you personally

Secret Poem

If the whole world blackballs me
Then I guess I will go live
on another planet called Black Ball
and it will be totally made of Onyx
except for the rivers and waterfalls of 7 Up
that flow near the caves
where me and my friends will play marbles
and maybe some billiards like maybe some 8 ball
and we will not talk about the blue green earth
because it is a loss so great
and a time so dark
for all those people.

Joke Policy

I try not to joke too much about rain
because what if it rains near a hospital.

poem

maybe heaven will be very similar to earth
but with a lot of rabbits everywhere you turn

poem

When people on other planets write science fiction
do they write about us?

Raging

People can hurt me for my mistakes but the weakness of God is stronger than the strongest human strength and in that same way with a breeze at my back maybe my cheesiest thoughts will be commemorated by pizza places in hell which are air conditioned and of course sell Italian ice.

Actually

A good defense on judgement day
might be to say that you were just joking

Anonymous

Sheila did not know where to sit at first when she got to the AA meeting. The group ended up putting the chairs in a circle and introducing themselves. When they got to her, she said, "Hi I am not really an alcoholic but I wanted to come to this meeting because I have another addiction which is trying to please people and use people to get attention for myself."

"Hi, Sheila," said the group leader. "this is an open meeting so you are welcome to be here but this is a group for alcoholics and that is not really the kind of addiction that we are here to help with."

"Honestly," said another member to Sheila, "I take offense to your using the group that way."

"Well for me it is a big problem, the way I just sign up for everything and do a lot of volunteer work to impress others," said Sheila.

"I don't understand how you could come here and compare that to what we have to deal with," said another group member.

People seemed to be getting mad, so Sheila decided to leave.

"I am going to leave," she said, "but before I do, do you guys mind posing for a picture for my facebook page?"

Go gentle into that great day

Rejoice, rejoice,
at the dying of the dark

Camoflauge

What they don't tell you in the army
is that the best camoflauge
is sitting in an actual pile of snakes.

One of my little social skills

If someone tells me something amazing
I tell them that I don't believe them.

Disorder

Thinking that you are important
can be a sign of psychosis
but I think that any Christian
who asks God for 10 million castles
is probably very important.

The eyes of Christ

The loving gaze of Jesus Christ
does not waver
and if one of my prayers
ever made him roll his eyes,
the planets would probably spin out of orbit
and the mountains would fall into the sea,
and that would probably only happen
if I prayed some kind of horrible prayer,
like if I asked for the planets to spin out of orbit,
or the mountains to fall into the sea.

I did think something of it at the time

I just thought hey I should have thought of that myself when the wind blew my food on the ground and the birds ate my waffle fries I felt happy and then I left and went and gave those people some money and had a great day like usual but then at night when it was dark and time to have a temporal lobe seizure or maybe not I thought okay wait a minute that food incident was a message from God saying feed the birds kind of like in Mary Poppins okay what is the secret message He is saying I am AM okay wait a minute and there was that fire flame in that window of the restaurant and was that Moses or Abraham that had that situation and okay I was frustrated when my food fell kind of like when Moses got mad when he was getting the ten commandments and the secret message says I need to not be as suicidal so much I need to do better and was God saying I was racist no he was saying he was not racist ok but is God saying he is morning or mourning and is it the same thing in the conspiracy I don't really know and okay if He is saying He is "being" does that have something to do with me being a sloth because I am a sloth I am a little baby sloth but I am that gray kind of sloth that is the kind of sloth I am okay He is also saying we are not a codfish well I do know what that means and that it might have something to do with the earth's burning core which I did think about recently and was he saying it was night and go towards the big building which I was pretending that my imaginary mice built over a long period of time by visiting Narnia a lot and the mouse in charge is Italian but the building has the same name as my old Protestant Church well honestly that confuses me a little bit and then the poetry reference but you know what I do see how maybe there weren't secret messages where God says he is going to magically pull a lamp out of a smaller bag and really it has nothing to do with Mary Poppins but was in fact just the wind blowing my bag of food off the table because it is fall and the weather is changing which okay wait a minute that is definitely a reference to Mary Poppins.

Maybe the people

Maybe the people I am judging
are carrying a torch to a next generation
but maybe that torch is wicked green fire.

Decoys

What if in heaven
everyone finds out
that the Catholic saints were just decoys
to keep everyone from realizing on earth
what kind of goodness was happening from regular people.

A little idea I had

I think a good question for a job interview would be
okay would you eat a cake that took five years to make?

You should not joke about this

What if a church decided to baptize everyone really fast
by running all the photos in the whole directory
through a Photoshop watercolor filter?

Really I am joking
and people should not count on that
but what if someone did do
a very good watercolor of a church?

Poem grocery store cars

This I promise you

I believe that within our life time
People will someday not drive to the grocery store
But instead every car will be a grocery store
And people will drive around in grocery stores
that probably also fly.
And people will look out their rear view mirror
and see the very day that this was predicted which is now
The grand opening of this poem
That foretold what was guaranteed to happen.
If this does not come true
I promise that I will personally
buy everyone their own grocery store car plane
if they are in fact available
and if I have enough money
from investing in grocery store car planes.

Barnes and Noble Barnes and Noble Barnes and Noble Barnes and Noble

In heaven there will probably be some Barnes and Noble stores
but there will also be Barnes and Noble Barnes and Noble stores
that don't just sell books
but sell Barnes and Noble Stores
so people can buy one
and have it delivered
to add on as a level to their house
or to add as a basement
or just to attach to their house or put in the backyard
and most people will have one
kind of like a lot of people have garages now
and it probably won't be staffed
but maybe people will go ahead and work part time
in each other's Barnes and Nobles,
or maybe there will be traveling employees,
who work shifts in everyone's bookstores,
until they finally come home
to the fifty level Barnes and Noble they live in
with the other employees,
where there are 50 million stories per story,
and a tunnel system
to help with the coffee recipe invention level,
and the little office for meetings,
which people would not suspect
is the headquarters
for all of the world
and all of the worlds.

Prayers

Yeah I do ask God to give people turbo boosts
of hope, and strength, and some kind of goodness,
because God help us,
some people don't do their chores.

poem

What if they had a service called Mean Maids
and it was people who come help you clean your house
and they come in and aggressively throw away everything you have?

Severe Genius

so smart they broke

poem

guys i did not mean to say God was a guinea pig.

I think that one poem I wrote does read that way

and I would like to apologize to God,

to all of Christendom,

to the United States of America,

to Jesus Christ and his disciples,

to Daniel and the lions from the lions den,

to Shadrach, Meshach, and Abednego,

and to Paul and all of the suffering missionaries all over the world.

I would like to apologize to my pet guinea pigs,

and to humanity for bringing shame on us all.

I would like to apologize to all of the microscopic aliens
watching us from their video portals
in the spaceships surrounding us
in the air we breathe,

and most of all, I would like to apologize
to the people at the pet store,

because really it is their fault, isn't it?

poem

What if you were writing someone a letter of recommendation to a social work therapy school and you spent the whole letter talking about your problems and then at the end mentioned that you do in fact recommend the student for social work school.

If I was a professor I would write a letter of recommendation like this:

Dear school,

    Skippy Jenkins is a sweet little baby frog and a class 5 sheep warrior who has not gone twenty days without working through the shop challenge. The code is 5588321. It is very simple. Please present authorization. I will tell you everything but what really matters is that Skippy will not be marked as downgraded on the element scale. Do not graph the grid document. Ok what the real situation is that if I was going to bake cookies for the people on the deserted island, I would be stirring the batter and I would remember that time Skippy said in class that he thought people could do what is right in a lose lose situation. That is what he said. I said I am sorry but I don't believe you. And then he showed me the map of Grantagne. And there is a lot I can't say in this letter, but I am sure you saw the news back in 1997 when they had those commercials for groove tubes. The kids were like "Groove Tube, groove tube, spinning around," and it worked. You know some things just work and that is why I would write down Skippy's name on the 55 form before stamping the other pictures. Ok but this is not a game. I can't break the lines or the treatment plan. Rx Risperdal if you know what I mean but this isn't about me.

    No need for a second paragraph but I will not back down I will not be pushed around I will not let a bunch of nary nary food swappers tell me what is right or wrong. Check the book on page 655 and you will see exactly what I am talking about. You want to look up a word in the dictionary? Look up the word ostentricious and do you know whose face will not be pictured? I guarantee you it will be Skippy Jenkins. Skippy 1 Skippy 2 Skippy Skippy me and you. Everything hangs in the balance and if you care at all about the future of radiometrics then you know what to do.

Recommend _____
Highly Recommend _X_
Recommend with mild threats _____

poem

If you think this book is too interesting
please pass it along to someone else.

poem

What if you went to a church
and the pastor said
"We should not be so proud of ourselves
as to think that we are not Satan."
You know what honestly I would probably
go to another church instead
because I do not think most of us probably are Satan.
I mean really that is one thing I think we
consistently have to be thankful for
is that we aren't the most evil creature
or at least a creature responsible for that much evil
that transcends time periods,
and I feel like it is not something
that makes me feel overly proud either,
you know I am bad sometimes
and who knows what all my little life decisions add up to,
but I don't think I am some kind of
dark prince or lord of an underworld
and I also don't go around bragging about it.
But I do brag sometimes so maybe I should be careful.

From on high

Sometimes the confusion is the wisdom
and people don't understand
because it doesn't make sense.
And it's okay to be scared of the Great Pumpkin,
but you don't have to be.

When I die

I will say you know what
I wanted some food
and I did what I had to do.

New York City

I went to the city
to live deliberately,
and to get away
from all those trees
that aren't people and buildings.

A Literary Idea

I think a great book would be
War and Peace all mixed up
and then you have to unscramble it.

Just something I noticed

There are bronze no smoking signs in some places
and in my neighborhood
there is a food guy that could charge
five dollars just for the smells
but he charges five dollars for the chicken.

I'll take the subway.

On the subway train
I noticed a price tag ground into the floor
and it said 99 cents.

Roger you are safe now.
Dave, Fred, you're going to be okay.

I know that Satan
would love to crush my pet guinea pigs
with a soccer cleat.
But that is not going to happen
as long as I keep feeding them,
giving them water,
and cleaning their cages.
People say "What made you think about that?"
Well I was just looking at Roger and thought of the worst.
And we really don't know that it hasn't already happened
and that these guinea pigs I have are just mechanical replacements.
But I think these guinea pigs are the same guinea pigs
I have always had,
and my apartment lease says nothing
about any portals
to a demonic underworld
that would give any evil principalities access to my pets.
People say, "Hey is something wrong
that is making you think of all these things?"
And as a matter of fact something did bother me yesterday.
I wanted to go see one of my favorite comedians get interviewed
and I mixed up the locations and missed it.
People say well maybe it would help
to hold a pet guinea pig for a while.
Yeah it does help a lot but you know what I am still worried
because there is not a toaster in my apartment you know
and surprising me with a free toaster is something
that a demon wouldn't do.

poem

Guys you know how there is such thing as "found poetry"
where people stumble upon some nice words and call it a poem
and there are "naturally occurring retirement communities"
where people just happened to make there be a retirement home
well what if there were such a thing as "found universities"
like where there is a zone where people read a lot
and share a lot of ideas or have too many parties?

poem

What if you couldn't afford a wedding ring
so you just gave your spouse ringworm?

poem

What if you got married to a person
who had been divorced
and you loved them a lot
and you photoshopped yourself into all their old family photos
and gave them their own old photo album for Christmas.

Do y'all think this poem is sacriligious?

What if you were flipping through the newspaper
and you realized that a particular grocery store ad
was the most profound Christian allegory
that the world has ever seen
and everyone started to study it in schools and churches
and it became the most famous work of literature
from the 21st century
and when the students thousands of years later learned about it
they were like wow that is a good price for detergent
and miracles start happening
and one of the miracles
is that they make a time machine to take tourists back to your time period and one of those people turns out to be the person who designs that grocery store ad.

poem

You need to be careful
telling everyone
that your imaginary pet mice are praying for them
because some people aren't believers.

poem

Call me crazy but I refuse to stay in psychiatric wards
where they have wallpaper with a snake design.

poem

Guys did y'all feel
like that dog at the park
already knew you?

Patient

What if you go out to eat
and at the restaurant
you're reading the menu
and the waiter asks you what you want
and you say I don't know
and he comes back ten or fifteen times
and you still don't know because it all looks so good,
and several hours pass,
and he comes back twenty or thirty more times,
and you start crying because you just can't decide,
and then a day or two passes and you are really hungry
and it isn't funny anymore but you just don't know what to choose
and they have to take you to the hospital
and at the hospital they ask you what kind of jello you want
but you wont know what flavor to ask for.

Just something I was wondering

If advertisers get paid to bother everyone
during their favorite shows,
shouldn't unemployed people get paid double
for leaving everyone alone?

poem

if people try to squelch you
maybe they are ashamed of you
or maybe they are ashamed of themselves in your bright light.

Praying Mantises

You gotta hate being a generation
that eats its young
and its young's young.

Super Earth

It seems like a simple choice at first
to choose between heaven or hell.
I easily trust God and choose heaven
and wonder how people can be so stupid.
But then later it's like okay
do I try to do great things
and earn a super heaven
or do I go with the basic heaven deal
and eat more chocolate here now.
You know honestly that's a tough one
except for the fact that I can't stop eating chocolate
no matter what
So it seems like the decision is already made
except then maybe when the chocolate is not enough,
and suffering gets ugly,
it's like okay I might be eligible
for some kind of really great reward,
but I also really need some relief,
so could I trade some super heaven later
for some basic heaven right now.
or even basic earth.
But people say well basic earth includes suffering.
And I say okay but are you sure this isn't basic hell.
And could I get some basic heaven now
in exchange for some super hell later.

Poem

I am thinking about
not eating a Reeses peanut butter cup this Halloween
as just an exercise in extreme self denial
like walking on coals
or like the very thought
of not eating a Reese's peanut butter cup this Halloween.

What's terrible

What's terrible is when you find out
that everyone who said "I like you"
was talking to your hat.

Subway

I think that when the subway drivers
let the doors close on me on purpose
that must be their way of giving me a hug.

Yeah I will say it

The bad people deserve for us to live down to their accusations.

poem

Is it rebellious to say to God
"the world has refused my services"
and then go play dominoes?

poem

You know how people do things in someone's honor
like say these flowers are in honor of this great person?
Well what if people hurt you
and you do something in shame of them?

Quandary

What if everyone has all always cheated at math and physics
and all numbers and equations actually don't mean anything at all

Free Advertising

I think a great brand name
for an airline would be "Probably Dangerous."

Pet Project

These are dangerous times
which means no playing around
but that won't stop me from being patient enough
to act suspicious in the train station
so the security dogs will visit me.

Relaxation Technique

When I am at the beach,
I get double relaxation
by closing my eyes
and pretending that I am at the beach.

Paradise

What if in heaven people live in giant renditions
of the sand castles they made as kids?

The angels think I'm stupid.

The angels think I'm stupid,
but that doesn't mean
they don't make the best of it
when I accidentally leave some blessings
for other people.

poem

people can call me a hypocrit
but they don't know what I had to grow out of
to get to false false humility.

poem

sometimes when things go great for people
they are disappointed
because what they really wanted
was for things to go wrong for everyone else.

poem

A lot of people would be heartbroken
or even devastated
to have a mental problem like mine
but I was able to adapt so well
that the people at church
thought it was just selfishness.

poem

At group therapy
everyone agreed
that when I catch all the mice in my apartment
it would actually not be that nice
to let them go at a deli nearby.

Diet Coke

What if there was a certain kind of coke machine
that took cokes away from people?

The Next Year Reindeer

At the North Pole, there is a friendly and soft reindeer named Rufus. He is a nice googly eyed deer who likes to wear Christmas lights in his antlers and has a lot of friends who are Christmas mice.

One year he heard about some situations in stores where they ran out of the toys that children wanted. The managers said to the people, "Maybe next year."

Soon after that, Rufus heard about some parents who wanted to buy some new furniture instead of toys for the kids. When the kids asked for the toys they wanted, the parents said "Maybe next year."

Rufus also went to a meeting with Santa and saw Santa look at a letter from a child who had only been a little bit good that year but was asking for a big toy. Santa put the letter aside and said "Maybe next year."

Rufus cried a little bit and went back to his stable. He talked to his Christmas mice friends and said, "I think these kids should get toys now. Will you guys help me?"

The Christmas mice said "Of course," and they hurried to fill up some bags with toys.

At about 9 oclock on Christmas Eve, way before he was supposed to join the other reindeer to pull Santa's sleigh, Rufus picked up the big bag of toys and dragged it through the snow. Then he and the mice hopped on a bus and started to deliver the toys. Everywhere he went, people petted him and thanked him.

It was almost midnight but he still had one toy left. He decided to take it to a little girl who had wanted a wonderful unicorn stuffed animal.

When Rufus got to her house, the little girl was sipping hot chocolate with her mom. Rufus gave her the unicorn and she and her mom both cried because they were so happy. They shared some hot chocolate with Rufus and all the mice and gave Rufus a plaid blanket to take home.

When Rufus got back to his stable at the North Pole, Santa and the other reindeer had already left to go deliver presents. A

Christmas bird said to Rufus, "Rufus, why aren't you flying with Santa and the other reindeer?"

Rufus curled up under his new blanket and said, "Maybe next year."

What's important

What's important
is that we impress
all the invisible rabbits
that hop all around us.

Why a light bulb is over my head

No one needs to call me
a technology wizard at this time,
but I have a little idea for an invention,
which is electric guitars powered by seizures.

Accommodations

I think kids taking tests
should have their choice
between using a calculator
and using one of those magic 8 balls.

Just wondering

If you decide to follow Jesus Christ
and then at the train station,
someone is walking in front of you,
does that mean that they are Jesus Christ?

Do I know you?

If I see someone who looks like someone I know I start to wonder if everyone is really a prototype for like a million people and there are a limited amount of people molds and if I have almost finished meeting everyone at least symbolically.

What if?

What if you get to heaven
and you have a job
and one of your bosses
is a little mouse?

another animals as bosses in heaven poem

What if in heaven
animals have jobs
and your boss turns out to be
the guinea pig from your childhood

Now Hiring

What if you wanted to work at a certain company
and they said well what job do you want
and you said "Employee of the month"
and they go okay
and they hire you as a permanent employee of the month
and your main job every day
is to walk around smugly.

A rude surprise

You know what I think wouldn't be a good idea?
I think it would not be good to go around
doing the opposite of pickpocketing
and sneaking up to people
and putting money in their pockets
because as nice as it is,
if you get caught,
they probably won't believe that's what you were doing.

poem

What if you sued your old bosses
for being mean to you
but then at the trial
it became apparent
that you had a hidden psychological
regression fantasy about your managers
and when they took the stand
you pointed to each of them
and you said "That's my mommy."
And then when you took the stand
you had a blanket and you go
"I want my mommy."

poem

this is just a poem to clarify
that I did not say Americas future didn't matter
or that freedom is a joke
or who cares if people don't know the words to their favorite song
which does not have to be the national anthem,
and i did not say that people weren't welcome
to visit me on thanksgiving
unless they bring something real yummy
 which does remind me to let everyone know
that there are some great recipes
if you just google cream cheese
but anyway if people think
that i am going to sit idly by
while millions sit idly by,
then they must have been sitting idly by
when the Christmas parade
marched through town throwing candy canes,
which aren't anything but a symbol
of all that is red and white,
and sometimes blue,
although not usually.

Guinea Pigs are Not God

You know who is a friend for me is someone
who walks down the street humming a song called
Guinea pigs are not God.
Because that is something I agree with
and I don't believe that guinea pigs died on the cross
for peoples sins,
except some guinea pigs do not get taken care of that well,
and they want some apple slices,
and what I am actually trying to say
is that I still have some chores left to do today
but do you know who is not going to judge me
when all is said and done?
Fred, Roger, and Dave.

Please explain your behavior.

guys I turned out a little sassier than people expected didn't I.
I think the intense nerdiness was actually part of the recipe
and cheese and sour cream also have to be part of it
because that is in almost everything I eat isn't it.

poem

The guinea pigs know

they can expect some food in the mornings.

There's a lot they know.

There's a lot they don't know.

The Feds

They are going to say
you bought Christmas presents
with the compounding loan
didn't you.
and I will say no
but I took some copyright liberties
and then they will say well that is why
Fred and Roger and Dave are being sent to China.

poem

It is not easy being a Christian
because you can't just
tell the bad people who hurt you
that you hope their souls
shatter into a thousand pieces
so they can burn in a thousand hells.

poem

People made things difficult
and I don't know what Judgement Day will be like for me.
Perhaps I will be given a strawberry scented bookmark
and a lava lamp.
Or perhaps I will be on the council that decides
hell is not enough.

Christmas Frog Poem

If people were smart
they would look in the mirror every day
and ask themselves
do I want to steal people's money
or do I want Jesus Christ
to say to me in front of all of humanity
that I am truly one of those Christmas frogs
from the best wrapping paper there ever was.

Therapeutic Job Interview

"Hi, Reggie, thanks for coming in to talk with me today," said Manager Fred. I have your resume here and your letter which says you are interested in being an assistant manager at our bookstore."

"Yes sir, that's right. I have been wanting to work here for a while and I have a lot of management experience from the frozen yogurt place where I used to work."

"And I see that you have some experience volunteering at a crisis phone line."

"Yeah I try to help people with mental health because I have had a hard time myself."

"Oh really?" said Manager Fred. "Thanks for telling me that. I used to be a counselor before starting to work retail. What seemed to be your main mental health struggles?"

"Well I get depressed because I feel like everyone is better than me. You know I try to show up for work and do my best but sometimes I just can't get everything done and certain things remind me of other failures. Like when I forget to lock the door to the cash office, it reminds me of other times that I have left registers unlocked and people have taken money from the businesses where I have worked.

"Hmmm... I see... tell me more about that..."

"Well I think that partially it is a fear of responsibility, you know, like maybe as a kid I just felt like I couldn't bear the responsibilities I had, which were to take care of my pets, but also sometimes to take care of my whole family, because my dad was distant in some ways, and my mom relied on me a lot emotionally."

"Hmm, I think you could be right about that. It sounds like you may still feel some anxiety, and it could be affecting you in ways you don't realize."

"Yeah, I do feel anxious and worried a lot. I think it makes me forgetful and makes me tend to do things randomly, like scheduling people on too many holidays, instead of going by company guidelines."

"Well that's certainly understandable, and I mean you can't blame yourself for every employee who quits or every hundred or thousand dollars of company money that you lose. I tell you what. Let's go ahead and sign you up for the job, and I think we should meet every week at first so we can keep discussing some of these issues. For next Friday I'd like you to please bring in two forms of I.D., and please also be prepared to tell me more about your mother."

A Nonfiction Article About Some Mice

This is a true story about some wonderful mice who helped a lonely person named Refried Bean.

Gusseppe was the first mouse to start helping Refried and being Refried's friend. Refried was in group therapy and felt ashamed sometimes so she started sending a big imaginary gray mouse named Gusseppe to leave the room and go take messages to people she knew. She sometimes sent Gusseppe out of the building to take messages to the person she liked.

It turned out that the person she liked also had a messenger mouse named Delores. Delores and Gusseppe decided to get married, so they both came to live with Refried in Refried's room. They would sleep on the bed in case Refried accidentally imagined scary snakes on the floor. Gusseppe and Delores had three kids named Flippy, Zippy, and Dippy. Dippy was born at the Cloisters monastery and museum, and everyone could tell there was something special about him. He had some special needs and a little bit of mixed up gender, but he also seemed to have some special art talent. He eventually married a little black mouse named Dafuskie.

As the little children mice were growing up, a special thin imaginary white labrador retriever named Soft Rover came to live in the apartment. Soft Rover was a rescue dog and would howl at night because of being scared. Soft Rover had a rough life before coming to the safe place and Delores would sing songs into Soft Rover's ear to help Soft Rover feel safe. She would sing "Soft Rover, Soft Rover, we love you so much and we're not going to hurt you."

Soft Rover calmed down and got a job taking Gus, Delores, the kids, and some other mice to the coffee shop. The mice would all sit in rows on a backpack that Soft Rover wore.

Some of the other mice included a tan mouse whose name was also Refried and who had two tan parents whose names I can't say because they are people that big Refried knows in real life. (Big

Refried is a person and not a mouse and is just being called Refried in this story.)

Anyway, there were also two brown mice named Buster and his wife. Buster is a rock star and very good at singing and songwriting. Buster has schizophrenia, and one time when Refried was at group therapy, a therapist served all the imaginary mice some imaginary steak dinners, and Buster rolled in the bernaise sauce and had to be washed off first from a mindfulness imaginary beach exercise, and later in a bathroom sink. He would walk around the therapy room telling everyone that it was his group and he was in charge but really everyone knew that was because of his mental health problems. Buster's wife was an art teacher at an art school in Refried's living room. The school was located near the couch where some imaginary ant eaters lived. The ant eaters helped all the mice when they felt upset and scared.

A lot of exciting things happened to the mice, and Refried would sometimes celebrate by getting them a pizza. At Refried's school, they had taught about social things like privilege and intersectionality of identities. Refried sometimes felt mad at the school and felt like people were blaming her for all of society's problems, but when she bought pizza for her imaginary mice, she realized that actually there was some instersectionality happening, because a big pizza to share with mice was a luxury, but to be so lonely that you imagine mice as friends could be a sign of a less privileged status.

Anyway one exciting thing that happened was that Flippy, who was Gus and Delores's first son, got accepted into med school and became the first mouse psychiatrist to work with humans. He did his internship at Columbia Doctors in downtown Manhattan, and later got a job at NYU Epilepsy center. Patients felt that they could trust him, and this was partially because he would whisper in people's ear that their medicine was not going to hurt them. It was kind of like the way his mom had whispered in Soft Rover's ear.

Refried Bean (the person) took a train to SC to go to the beach in August, and at the train station, there was a thin black lab who helped police by sniffing bags. Soft Rover and this dog fell in love and got married. So Soft Rover and the dog lived on Refried's bed along with several mice families. At the beach, some dolphins rescued some black mice from Dafuskie Island, and these mice also came to live at Refried's apartment. The mice were members of a church that Gusseppe and Delores had started, and they eventually became the leaders after Gusseppe got worn out and went to carpentry school.

The mice from Dafuskie island started posting songs on youtube, and because of this, they reached many more people and had a church with a lot of members from different places.

All of the mice's lives were changed forever one day when Refried took them all to the Cloisters museum and monastery, because it turned out that there was an entry way to Narnia there. Narnia is a place mentioned in C.S. Lewis's books, and it is kind of like heaven and very magical.

The mice were able to go back and forth from Narnia and come back to Refried's apartment through her wooden drawers, and by going back and forth to Narnia very frequently, Gusseppe was able to build many amazing buildings over time. One of the buildings he built is downtown and is so cool. It is one of the most well known skyscrapers in New York City.

Refried and the mice were all living their lives and getting along great when a little white mouse asked Refried for some cheese. Refried realized that this mouse needed a family so the mice from Dafuskie island adopted the mouse and named her Milky. Milky was so sweet and would sing a song in people's ears that is from the Care Bears and it says "Someone cares for you..." Milky loved to sing this song, and she sang it to a mouse that she liked named Cookie. Cookie was a black and brown mouse and he grew up to be a cook. They got married very young and had some calico kids. Cookie often confronted people and would sing something like "What's going on in such and such place" when he was in a situation that seemed like there might be a problem. He was very brave and did the best he could every day. He works at Mcdonalds and tried to help a lot of younger mice get internships and jobs there.

Something crazy happened one day, which was that Milky and Cookie adopted 300 orphaned mice and built two children's homes for them. Later there were three boarding schools for the mice, which included a school like Hogwarts, a Christian school in the mountains of laundry in Refried's room, and then a comedy school. This was all in addition to the art school. The mice were very special and got a lot of comfort and healing and went on a lot of field trips.

One of the reasons that the mice could take care of all the little children mice at the schools is because they had some help from some rabbits. A rabbit named Reuben and his wife named Mister took care of a lot of the mice at Hogwarts, and Reuben kept helping even after he got in trouble because people accused him of smoking. But he was not smoking. He was eating a banana. Later he got schizophrenia but Buster let him be in his band and he still helped out at the school. Reuben and Mister had a son named Parsnip who wrote stories. Parsnip got married to a mouse named Juniper. All of the mice and rabbits helped out at the schools, and the mice from the school started growing up and using all of their many gifts and talents.

One of the mice from Delaware began singing songs to people on the subway and then got married to a mouse that helped him and wore a similar scarf as him. They sang songs with the words "I love you, I just want you to know that I love you."

Things got a little confusing when Refried discovered real mice living in her apartment, but all of the imaginary mice welcomed the real mice and Refried loved them all very much.

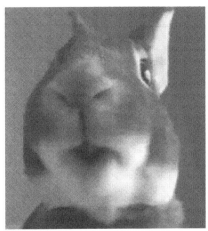

My Pet Died on Christmas: Blog Posts by Refried Bean

This is just a short collection of some of my posts from the blogs I started soon after e-publishing several books. Some of them are jokes, and some are serious, and some are opinions that might be wrong.

I would like to dedicate this book to Fred, Roger, and Dave. You are the best guinea pigs anyone ever had and I appreciate the way you guys are always there for me.

"...look, and see our disgrace.... we must buy the water that we drink.."
    Lamentations 5

New Blog and New Books

Hi everyone, I am starting a new blog and this is the first post. I used to have about ten blogs but deleted most of them. I posted a lot of poems on blogs, and some joke candy reviews. I recently published some e-books full of those poems, and some art and jokes and a novel on a site called smashwords. The books are also available on ibooks and the barnes and noble website. Here is a link to all the books so far: https://www.smashwords.com

Introduction

Hi everyone I am treating this blog like a journal and might post some art and poems and other ideas on another blog. Should I do an introductory post or should I just start a journal entry? I think I will say some stuff about myself.

I just moved to New York City three years ago after working in a bookstore for twelve years. About 30,000 people were mean to me at that bookstore, and I couldn't take it anymore, so I quit and came to NYC for social work school. It seems crazy to try to do a social job after breaking down so much from painful social interaction, but I felt like the degree would help me as a writer and would help me help other people who have suffered in ways that I have. I do think it was a good idea, and most of all, it was my ticket to New York City, where I can ride the subway and not drive a car anymore. I do not drive anymore because I feel too mad and also have some odd little space outs that I think could get worse.

With my insurance from social work school, I got some of the best medical care ever, including a video EEG, an MRI, awesome weekly group therapy for over a year, and the best individual art therapy anyone ever had. My mental health diagnosis has been straightened out some, and hopefully most of my problems are due to just a common case of Aspergers and Schizoaffective Disorder. I think it could be much worse, and when I say that, I mean both that I am thankful for things that are okay and I also mean that it might actually be worse and there might be an additional neurological condition that is causing memory and mood problems.

Anyway I am thankful to still be alive, because really I have had a rough time for a while, but I finished school and just published a whole bunch of e-books full of all my writing from the past ten or fifteen years. I think things turned out pretty good, and I am still writing new stuff and will keep going as long as I can.

A post about cookies

Guys people have concerns about various things involving social identity okay and before I go further with this blog I just want to let all my family and friends know that I identify as... Cookie Monster.

Early Retirement

Do y'all remember my 401K? I remember it. I spent it mostly on food and insurance. You know what I think would confuse people is if you donated disability checks to Republican party campaign funds. I mean wait a minute you know wait a minute that might create an explosion of some kind honestly like is it even safe that I typed it I am not sure. But anyway you could cash the check and then donate it as a little prank and they would never know and they would be at the podiums saying stuff and you would laugh secretly to yourself knowing that their foundation was crumbling underneath them almost as fast and thoroughly as liberty and justice.

Job Search Update

Hi everyone I wanted to tell y'all that this week I think I am going to a Voc Rehab office in New York. It is known as Access VR and I am hoping that they will help me find a food service job where I wont get fired after a week or even a day when people see that I talk to myself and can't make eye contact. I am hoping to get a job somewhere stirring batter and chocolate and then washing dishes later. It seems like there should be better job options for me, but I don't think there are. I just finished social work school, but honestly I didn't do that well except for a few papers that didn't seem to offend anyone as much as my fashion and hygiene problems did.

My favorite TV show

Hi everyone, what is your favorite TV show? My favorite show is Chopped. It is a cooking contest where people get random ingredients and have to think of a dish that uses all of those ingredients. They can use other ingredients too. It is a great show and I love to watch it on my computer. This is a good blog post isn't it. I mean I just said what I had to say which is that Chopped is my favorite show.

Guinea Pig Adventures

Guys, where's Roger!?!?! Just joking. He is in his cage. I wanted y'all to think that my guinea pig went missing. No, really, he is okay everyone. That was a mean little trick wasn't it. Sorry everyone. Please send cash. No I am joking again but really I do need to get a job soon.

Pancakes

You know what would be great right now is some pancakes but it looks like I am writing this blog post instead of cooking doesn't it.

Just to be Funny

Sometimes I really look forward to heaven everyone. I think there will be rolling green hills and stone castles and maybe kind of like restaurants there will be lots of fairs with some booths selling cotton candy and sno cones and nachos. And people wont have to be trapped in bad situations with bills and chores unless they want to just as a joke.

Hot or Cold

Something interesting that is happening in my life right now is that my refrigerator is broken and making a loud buzzing noise. It actually reminds me of the fire drills from elementary school. Those fire drills made me cry because they were so loud, and really this refrigerator situation also makes me feel a little bit like crying. But I am not crying, because I know that if I get used to the buzzing sound, it will help me be less bothered by the noise when I pull the fire alarms in my apartment building so I can go get cheese and sour cream from other people's refrigerators.

Hurricane Relief

Hi everyone, a hurricane is passing nearby right now. The news people told us to be careful but it is not even raining and the forecast says it will be sunny all week so I am not being that careful. I am just walking to the coffee shop and sometimes being thankful that the hurricane did not hit us. Something I was thinking about though is what if a hurricane hit somewhere and then came back a few years later to bother everyone again? Or what if it went to another location but one of those storm chaser people was there and recognized it and was like wait a minute, this is Hurricane Hugo from 1989.

What do y'all think of this blog post?

Hi everyone i felt like doing a blog post right now. What should i write about. How about how I am holding a sweet little guinea pig named Fred. Fred is so sweet and if you don't think so then maybe you should not have bought Fred. And now you say you didn't buy Fred and that he is my guinea pig and you don't have anything to do with it. Hmm. That is interesting but it confuses me because I have Fred right here and if you didn't buy him and I did, then why is he at your house right now. Oh okay he is here with me so he is not at your house. You know when people try to confuse me it makes me wonder if they are trying to get money from me, maybe so they can try to buy a guinea pig named Fred. And that makes me wonder if they are trying to actually buy this particular guinea pig as if he is not a guinea pig I picked out for myself. So please explain to me again why you are trying to tell me about your guinea pig named Fred when really he is sitting here safe and sound or so I thought. Honestly I am thinking about calling the cops and I have the evidence right here which is Fred and how sweet he is.

Yesterday's post

There was a bombing in New York today but I think most of the injured people are going to be okay. On the news they didn't say a whole lot about it except to describe the type of bomb and explain how it is made, I guess in case anyone doesn't know how. Anyway today I went and got some food in my neighborhood and there was a back pack near my door but I did not call the cops because it just wasn't that suspicious to me. I think it belonged to one of the guys playing dominoes out on the sidewalk and I don't think those guys are planning to hurt anyone unless they cheat at dominoes. But anyway something I am trying to figure out is okay if a terrorist is not a citizen then is it an act of war. Or what if an act of war is from a citizen. I think it is up to me right now on this blog to figure out but I am not even going to try because it will make my head explode and we have had enough explosions for the day.

A blog post

Hi everyone, today is the day after a bombing in NYC. I just got back from getting coffee in my neighborhood and checking a certain subway location to make sure everyone was safe there. I was worried that it could be a target but they seemed to have a lot of security. I also made sure not to go appliance shopping because really I think I could seem suspicious carrying something that looks like my broken air conditioner which does seem like it could be part of a very strategic plot against me and society at large.

One more thing

I just want to say one more thing about the bomb situation which is that those terrorists aren't going to scare me into leaving my apartment and getting stuff done or going about my daily business.

Also I had a little joke which is what if after there was a bombing in a trashcan you went around diving onto any piece of trash you saw on the sidewalk and were like "everybody get back!" and threw yourself onto a coke can or a plastic chip bag or something and kept doing it all along your walk down the street.

This post is about ice cream and isn't about the bombing from a few weeks ago

Hi everyone, something reminded me of a happy memory that I wanted to write about on this blog. It is a memory of how one time at McDonalds I went through the drive through and ordered either a hot fudge or caramel sundae (I think it was hot fudge) and the person put the fudge sauce on the bottom and the top of the sundae. Usually you only get the sauce on top. I do not know how much they were or were not allowed to do that but it was a great surprise and I will always remember it until I have severe memory loss that makes me wander into a McDonalds and ask for a sundae with all hot fudge and a little bit of ice cream on the bottom and the top.

A Mouse Named Nicey

Hi everyone, did y'all know that there is a mouse living in my apartment right now? There could be more than one but so far I am just guessing that it is one friendly little mouse that has no intention of scampering over me when I sleep. I have seen the mouse four times and it is so cute. I put out some water for it and I am going to try to catch it in humane traps. What should I name the mouse? Let's have a contest real quick to decide. Okay who thinks I should name the mouse "Herbert?" Okay... three people. Okay who thinks I should name the mouse "Nicey?" Okay...one..two... okay... Fifteen people have voted for me to name the mouse "Nicey." Ok thanks everyone. "What if there are a lot more mice in your apartment?" you ask. Well that could be quite a challenge to name a lot of mice and that is a lot of little hats and scarves to knit for Christmas isn't it?

Happy Halloween

Hi everyone I am very excited because Halloween is in just a few days and I have a lot of candy to pass out in my neighborhood, which usually has hundreds and hundreds of kids trick or treating. I think only one bag of the candy I bought is probably from last year, and it is all stuff I am willing to eat too. For my costume I am going to be a person passing out Halloween candy, which is definitely a costume because on most days during the year I don't pass out Halloween candy.

Missing Blog

Guys I was updating blogs today and noticed that one of my blogs seems to have disappeared. It was the art blog. Has anyone seen it? Maybe it ran away and it will be discovered accidentally when someone googles a recipe or something, like a refried bean recipe. But for some reason it is not on my link list anymore. I don't think it had any information that needed to be censored, or to be the opposite of censored, which would mean being hacked and distributed by Wikileaks.

Fried Bananas

Hi everyone, today is a Sunday in November. I wanted to share a little recipe because I just successfully made this food and it was so yummy. The recipe is called Fried Bananas. You heat up butter and sugar and cut a banana into fourths, you know, like cutting it length ways and in half, etc. Then you put those slices in the browning butter and sugar and it caramelizes. I think it is best if it is pretty hot. And then you put the cooked bananas over ice cream and then you eat it and feel a little bit proud, possibly to the point of arrogance and with some snootiness that becomes permanent. It's kind of nice after some taco salad or bean dip and limeade.

Can't Get Too Thankful

Hi everyone. Today is Thanksgiving. I am having a little trouble today because I am taking new psychiatric medicine that makes me feel guilty. I think it is kind of funny for the emotion to be so specific like that. It is like a plot for a story I might have written, where someone takes medicine that makes them feel guilty and they have to figure out what is right intellectually without their intuition and conscience working correctly. Well that is interesting isn't it, but I am okay. I am cooking some rice right now. I decided not to get a rotisserie chicken because I just didn't want chicken today so I think that is kind of like pardoning a turkey like Obama does on Thanksgiving. But I am not trying to make everyone else feel guilty for eating turkey or chicken. If I wanted to do that I would bring over an Abilify casserole.

Little Known Fact

Hi everyone I wanted to share a little known fact about myself which is that I invented basketball and the Apple Watch.

Partridges and Cartridges

Hi everyone. I hope y'all are having a great Christmas. I am but it is only December 17 so there is still time for me to fall down some stairs. I feel really happy about the presents I am giving this year, although the classic Nintendo game set with 30 games was not really rolled out in time for me to buy it this year for me or others. But I am okay and I have gotten lots of presents and have found that packing them in boxes is kind of like winning Tetris.

Oh, no you go ahead, no you

Hi everyone, today is Christmas Eve. On the way into my apartment building this afternoon, I tried to hold the door for this kid but he was trying to hold another door for me. It was kind of like O. Henry's Gift of the Magi Story and hopefully the security cameras got it on video so it can be on the Hallmark Channel every Christmas from now on.

Posts from Mad Blog

Three things I am mad about right now:

The way Papa Johns requires all job applicants to sign an agreement waiving their rights to settle disputes in the American court system and instead promises to let any work problems be resolved by a private arbitration company paid by Papa Johns. ("Pizzeria Law")

The way Bank of America thinks it is perfectly okay to hold checks for seven days before the money is available and also refuses to cash their customers' tax refund checks from the United States government.

Stores and restaurants that deliberately play bad music as loud as they can in order to speed up store traffic and get customers to leave faster.

Okay 147 and 91, not 119, okay why is there an adding machine

Hi everyone, I want to tell y'all about a little scuffle I recently had at a hotel. I was trying to go somewhere cool during the heatwave because I did not have air conditioning. I go in and I say hi the computer rate said such and such well do you have anything cheaper and they are like yeah but you have to make your reservation at those phones over there. (They did not want to do a transaction in person.) So I go to the phones and they say okay how about 119 per night. I go okay and pay with credit card. They say okay it is non refundable. (that is why they did not want to do it in person.) So then I go to check in and the guy wants me to sign a screen saying the rate is 147. Well that is not what they told me so I try to cancel. They say it is too late we already charged you and you are checked in. I say I am not staying here and I will not take the key and I think it is unreasonable to not let me cancel when I made the reservation ten minutes ago and you are telling me a different rate. So then I talk to the manager and he says okay you can cancel but your name is going to go on a list for twenty years. And he says the refund money will not show up in my account for a few days. So anyway there is a charge on my electronic bank statement saying 380 which was a hundred more than the deal was supposed to be and then a few days later it doesn't get refunded but simply disappeared. So I think they did some kind of wheeling and dealing with a bank in a way that did involve me getting my name put on a list or was he talking about my credit rating and called it a list to be deceptive. If so that is over 7 lies that took place during that whole transaction where no one would have a normal conversation with me. I have not checked my credit rating I mean do I have to buy a credit report from trying to get out of the heat for two days and then not being able to? Anyway I might wait until there is a problem and then get a lawyer. I have a screenshot of the charge that disappeared. Hotel Pennsylvania, see you on Judgement Day.

Not Nice

A few years ago, I noticed that Keebler had copied the girl scout cookie recipes, and I was a little shocked, because okay, those are supposed to be girl scout cookies. Today I noticed that the Walgreen's "Nice" brand has also copied them. So I guess that is that, you know, because recipes I think are considered public domain and do not have copyrights. I do think that is a good policy and yet wow I thought maybe people would go ahead and let the girl scouts have something special and seasonal. And another thing that bothers me everyone is the fact that probably I will eventually break down and buy some of those caramel delights I mean of course I will and the peanut butter patties and yeah ok the thin mints, and they know I will, you know all those ad wizards and marketers and food sharks, they know that I will not be able to stay loyal to the girl scouts. And it is true that the girl scout cookie industry became such big business that it is hard to see it as just little kids selling cookies anymore, which might be part of it too, and maybe this final acquisition, I mean copying, of the girl scouts is some kind of representative decision and conclusion that the girl scout cookie business can't honestly be called a fundraiser anymore and is part of a gillion dollar food industry. But I am kind of sad to see it happen, and I am also sad to see pretty much all those other Keebler brands and any other well marketed food brand to now have a store brand competitor product next to it for cheaper. So basically the stores with the power to decide shelf space get to squeeze out the brands that first developed the food products. But maybe this, too, is a representative decision and conclusion that those days of power are over for those brands, and now people have other ways to decide what to eat. This also could be related to another market trend of rejecting all those brands with preservatives and making room for the organic foods and hippie market. That was crazy of me to say hippie wasn't it, especially when all those people might have saved the day for everyone with food allergies. Anyway, I am rambling a little bit, and maybe some other people have cracked the code on all of this, and I can see how I haven't really made a single clever joke like I would have hoped to do in a post like this. But maybe that is because it really isn't funny to me, and my brand loyalty actually goes far enough to care about the people behind the brands, who I think might not be getting the merit badges they deserve.

Now is the time

It is election time and something that is very apparent is that many people in this country have a problem pretending that they live in different time periods. People act like we live during the American Revolution, they act like it is World War II and the Holocaust, they act like it is 1965, and some people even seem to think they are living during the Protestant Reformation. The best people out of all of them are the people who think they live in an Ayn Rand novel, and I think they are the truest Americans there are besides the Mexicans. But it is crazy to be fighting pretend fights with all that is actually happening and people have opportunities to literally save the world through basic human decency.

Bad News

I read the news a lot online and today and yesterday was reading it a little extra and I am a little upset everyone because I think there are some problems with a lot of our news. I usually read NBC news online because Fox news has a lot of pornography in the margins and the New York Times is complicated in a way that makes me wonder if maybe they don't really want me to understand what is going on. Anyway I read NBC and I feel so upset so often because of so many problems with that site. In addition to editorialized headlines that sound like middle school gossip, they often have videos where you can tell they have chosen to present those stories as videos because there is something horrible that probably should not be watched and made public. And yet that is the appeal they are counting on. It goes so far as to include stories about other news agencies posting inappropriate videos, and the story is basically something like "Can you believe this other news station posted this video of two heroin addicts passed out while their child was sitting in the car with them?" And then they show the video clips with an abused and neglected child sitting there online for everyone to see them in their moment of horror. Another terrible thing on the site is the "sponsored news" where it is a supposed news article but paid for by an advertiser. And yesterday after the bombing in New York City, there was a sponsored news article featuring... New York, New York, like maybe trying to get some accidental clicks from people trying to find out what was going on. The article was really about a random product other than their usual credit card companies advertising for student loans by talking about people who won millions of dollars or got rich quick in some way. This is all mixed in with their normal headlines, and these things are part of their news page every single day. An article I missed is any kind of reporting of ethical journalism being a thing of the past. I don't know how I would have missed that story if they had reported it, unless maybe it was in the middle of that video they posted "about" the bystanders watching someone being assaulted repeatedly on the beach.

Bordering

In one of my other posts, I mentioned Mexicans, and I don't know if I got it right, or if it came across wrong, but I want to say that I think that the both the greatness and the suffering of the Mexicans is right in our faces and there is no excuse and hasn't ever been an excuse to not do everything we can to welcome them and help them. If anything should be built on the border it is not a wall but maybe a few more statues of liberty.

Three Opinions about High School and College Grading

There should be diplomas all along the way for every year so students don't lose everything by dropping out in eleventh grade.

The lowest grade possible on any assignment should be a 50.

Failing grades should not go on transcripts or especially be calculated in GPAs. Bad grades should be dropped and the student should simply not get credit for the class.

Ok I have one more to add which is that it should be normal for 4 year bachelor degrees to be broken into sections that include a two year associate's degree.

People on their feet all day are sitting ducks.

Everyone knows these are dangerous times with absurdly random bombings and shootings, which should be the final straw that keeps the billionaire losers from underpaying all the service employees who work with the public. It was one thing when everyone complained about waiting in a long Wal Mart line for twenty minutes to pay a cashier that they all knew had to stand there for 8 hours without being able to afford basic food and shelter, but now people are literally risking their lives to take people's groceries to their cars. These workers should get paid for their time, and paid also for the other thing that people somehow don't see: their effort. There can't really be any reason that everyone would want to pay cashier salaries twice by paying retail prices, and then paying again with taxes for food stamps, unless maybe watching everyone get underpaid makes some people feel better about being on the wrong side of the counter.

Do y'all think we not see?

The liberal media is working hard to use Trump to make Christians in this country seem and feel like Nazis, but the fact is that the same media chose both candidates. There almost shouldn't even be a vote. The news people should just write their story or their screenplay and save everyone billions of dollars, or maybe not even write the story and waste readers' time but do something even more efficient, which would be letting the people who work at news stations automatically be the electoral college.

Rough Draft

Something that hasn't been in the news as much as people trying to associate me with the sins of political candidates is that Congress has been working on a bill to require all young American women to sign up for the military draft which now includes front line combat. I find it shocking and I think I don't agree with it, but am especially surprised to not hear people talking about it, because this is an issue that I would think might be the final straw for a lot of people, and that I think would make them decide to have their own military draft against people who would try to send their daughters to go be tortured by ISIS.

Do I work at CVS and if so would I get a paycheck?

At CVS there is a sign on the refrigerated waters that says to check the expiration date, which actually might be good advice for people who don't know, but I also am kind of like okay wait a minute isn't that your job CVS and are you trying to make me responsible for that in case someone messes up? I mean I am just wondering because I also noticed that the cashiers at that store sometimes run two registers at a time.

Terms and Conditions

Have you guys noticed that these store membership programs are becoming more complicated and they are now calling them "accounts?"

An Opinion about Eggs Benedict That Doesn't Seem Important But Maybe It Is

I know that I have some very serious topics on this blog but I did think it was also a good place to mention another opinion that I have which is that I think Eggs Benedict, which is usually a poached egg, hollandaise sauce, Canadian bacon, and an English muffin, would be much better if it was served with a biscuit instead of an English muffin and I have in fact tried it that way at a great restaurant and it was in fact much yummier. And I think all Eggs Benedict should be like that and I am considering inventing a new Google capability where you can google something and edit all occurrences of that text at one time and change all existing Eggs Benedict recipes to use biscuits instead of English muffins and now it seems that we have gotten to a more serious issue and I have actually scared myself a little and I am wondering if Google has already taken over more than I realized and edited my own DNA without me realizing it.

A nonmiracle not on 34th street

Hi everyone, I hope you all are about to have a Happy Thanksgiving. I am definitely going to have a Happy Thanksgiving, partially because of a free real life holiday special that my apartment property management company created. Today, everyone in my building got a letter informing us that they installed a new burner! That is just what I wanted for Christmas, and they are only charging us one entire month's extra rent for it! It is such a surprise, because it does not match the lease I signed, you know, and it seems like maintenance like that might be part of owning a building and charging people to live there. But what could be more heartwarming than literal heating maintenance in an apartment that I agreed to only pay twelve months rent for each year. The most exciting part about it is knowing that I might be making Christmas extra special for the real estate people, and that my extra rent could help the rich people buy that special Christmas present they want, like a full size working model of one of the twelve remote control cars I could have bought for Toys for Tots with this month's additional 93 dollars I have to pay in rent.

Eating gold is not cool.

I try not to judge people for things that aren't child abuse, but today I was at a fancy mall snack shop and they had desserts with gold flakes on top. Like real gold that you are supposed to eat. People can say that is no different than going to a fancier restaurant than necessary and splurging a little on some food but I think that it is. I think that it is basically an in your face dare for people like me to call it offensive and I will accept that dare and say that it is the flakiest thing I have ever seen or heard of.

I do not need Hibachi white sauce to be happy.

Today I went to a Hibachi restaurant and it was so fun but there was no white sauce and there was no white sauce at this other Hibachi restaurant I went to a couple of weeks ago but I am thankful for what I have and for what goes right in my life. But there was only a mustard sauce and a ginger sauce and it seemed like maybe the restaurants thought that too many people liked the white sauce and it was not there but I still think the meal reminded me of Thanksgiving because I am thankful for what I have. And maybe they felt that white sauce would have been so good that it was distracting. That I would understand because the white sauce really makes the meal in places like that but maybe they didn't want to be "a place like that" but instead more of a place that doesn't have white sauce.

Posts from the Worldly Monk Theology Blog

Worldly Monk Concept

Water and mud make bricks, especially under the sun, which can be useful for foundations of glorious kingdoms or humble havens. I feel that a water and mud comparison to what I have experienced helps me view my opportunities with hope as I have learned to make the most of being thoroughly overcome by what has to be the most disgusting culture that has ever existed. My mind and my soul and my life and environment are covered in the grime of this world, and in about years three and four of working at a Barnes and Noble for a long time, I started to accept this reality and decided to take every advantage I could to pray well in this condition. I have heard people talk about "trappings" before, and how people can sometimes escape the distractions and burdens of life and find sanctuary in places like the mountains or ironically to a "desert" to find rest and spiritual oasis. I have some memories of places like that from when I was a kid, but as an adult, I have found the true traps that people have set to be inescapable, horrifically violating, and burdensome in a soul crushing way that I do not expect to ever recover from in this life. Keeping insurance was the killer for me, but there are other traps in our culture, like the constant threat of debt and bad credit, low wages and high rent, email and personal information scams, unavoidable terrible music, disgusting movies that starve millions for satisfying storylines, and terrible news headlines about other people being violated in far worse ways. I almost can't take it at all, but over time have found great hope through prayer, and am so appreciative of all my links to humanity that retreating seems like it would be the least pure and good thing I could do. I am starting this blog as a place to share some reflections about what I have learned along my nasty, briar filled mud trap sand spur path, and I hope that people can find some happiness in a field of wildflower ideas grown with all the water that my shattered bucket could never hold.

Thanks Anyway

You know what is a section in the Bible that confuses me a little bit? It is the part where Jesus tells people about a guy who was proudly thanking God for not being as bad as other people, and then told about a guy who publicly said "Lord have mercy on me, a sinner," or something like that. Then Jesus says that God prefers the humility of the groveling sinner. I found that verse comforting during my worst depression where I felt so horrible and guilty all the time, but I often want to thank God for all the horrible things that have not happened in my life, and it confuses me a little bit that maybe we aren't supposed to. Like maybe we aren't supposed to thank God for not being one of those bad Isis people or a child abuser or something like that. I think the idea is that we don't know all the consequences of our every day behavior and the loss of the good we haven't done but could have. But I am thankful that I have not done worse things than I have, and especially as someone with mental illness and anger problems, I don't take it for granted that there are a lot of crimes I have not committed. So I have kind of decided that I will go ahead and thank God for all the ways that things could have been worse for me, including the category of my own behavior, and maybe if I thank him too much every time there is a shooting that I didn't do, then I will eventually feel so bad about my pride that I will say more things like "Lord have mercy on me, a sinner."

For other people with monk tendencies

I just have a few thoughts for this post which is about appetites and hunger. Sometimes when people really want to be a good person and pray a lot and accomplish some kind of great service and sacrifice, they try to be strict and disciplined in many ways. Jesus did say to deny yourself and following Christ does involve great sacrifice in a way that is often habitual. But everyone needs love and attention and food and happiness. People can get frustrated by hunger and find that it interferes with their lifestyle goals and doesn't keeps them from being as strict or dedicated as they wanted to be, or maybe... seem. But I have found that appetites can actually be some of the best things we have going for us as we try to live a good life and do what we are supposed to. Appetites can keep us honest and connected to others, and relatable. Going ahead and letting yourself get some attention and eat some yummy food not only keeps you happy and healthy enough to serve people well, but it can be an act of service itself, or put you in the situations where you see other people's needs that you can help with. Most of all, it can prevent the hypocrisy of always trying to seem better than people. If eating a big plate of food with a friend or hero can be the greatest secret weapon against one of the worst sins, I would say that is the deal of a century and from now on I am only going to read my Bible if I get ice cream too.

How Good

One time I read a book about the categories of Catholic saint characteristics and qualifications. I can't remember all the categories that the book focused on, but some of them included teaching and influence, suffering and self denial, service, like to the poor, and maybe one or two more. I wondered at the time why creativity wasn't a category, since that is also a witness of God's nature, and recently I thought that a specific type of suffering, like humiliation, could have been considered a factor. Most of all, I think that everyone who tries to do what they are supposed to in life has a mix of these things in their lives, and people do not always know what everyone's true sacrifices or suffering is. So even though I think it can be good to pick some superheroes and say okay everyone, "'this person got it right," I think I side with the Protestants in thinking that asking Christ's perfection to count for them puts everyone on a path of glory where almost anything in their lives will be some kind of demonstration of God's goodness, even if it includes things like failure at being good, and grief about that failure.

Fame and Glory

This post is something I figured out along the way and I think that for certain people who have certain sets of sinful tendencies, it could really save your life or your church's life. I think it is especially helpful for people who are a little bit attention seeking like I am. Basically I noticed as I grew up and tried to follow all the great teachings from church and the Bible, that some of the worldly attitudes and habits that Christians are supposed to avoid can actually be somewhat unavoidable in a way that makes people choose the option of pretending. And what I am saying is that even with basic intentions to not be overly concerned with things like fame, wealth, and power, these ambitions often just get transferred to Christian settings instead of denounced entirely which is most people's intention. So people who do mean well decide not to spend their efforts on making a lot of money or trying to be famous, and they try to instead live a life of humble service. That is great and that is the Christian life. But I think it is hard for some people to not go ahead and pursue that extra love and attention and even a search for money but in a setting where all the other rules are Christian. So they build their empire as a church volunteer. I mean really it can still mostly benefit people and an ambitious church can be a great gift to the community. But I am saying that personal desires to be known in a certain way and to have a comfortable life play out in a Christian setting and kind of intrude it with something that was supposedly going to be different than all those bad people on TV. So what I think is the answer is for some people to go ahead and try to go after their ambitions in a more worldly sense and go ahead and be rich and successful in the way that many Christians have denied themselves. I am saying that people with some tendencies are better off just going for the worldly fame and glory and that ultimately, even with judging Christians looking on, in their souls they will be more honest and the church will be preserved. And maybe they can give some cash later, and maybe they have an outreach that even they do not realize.

Actors, find a stage.

This post is very similar to the one I just wrote, but I wanted to say something else I have learned as a person with acting skills and attention seeking behavior. I think that if people have acting talent and have a tendency to play out characters in some kind of Christian sense where you are spending energy on trying to seem a certain way, then a way to immediately fix it is to find some kind of theatre hobby where you actually do acting. I am talking about plays, skits, and stand up comedy. I think that makes people be themselves in other settings where it is tempting to exaggerate something like goodness, or kindness, or anything else admirable. People might say well maybe the acting kind of people don't have to be themselves. Well, some people do struggle more, and maybe acting a little bit here and there is being themselves, but God does mostly tell us to be ourselves.

Harnessing Hypocrisy

It is crazy for me to post this post so soon after my post about going ahead and letting your achievement be outside the church but I have this other idea that I have learned from my struggles with motives. Even though sometimes you really can't do stuff with mixed motives, there are other times where it is more important to get the work done than to have some kind of pure unselfish heart, and the tendencies to want credit and attention can be used in your favor to just get more service out of yourself. What I am saying is just go ahead and be a hypocrit and get the hungry people fed. And flamboyantly drop the hundred dollar bills in the offering plates in front of everyone.

Three thoughts at Christmas

Having some bad feelings every now and then doesn't mean that there is a demon attached to your face, and a milkshake might do the trick.

Christmas is a great time to reward good behavior but it probably shouldn't be turned into a Judgement Day for children.

Everyone wants a remote control car and a puppy.

Tripwatch Overlay:
A Book About Prayer

by Refried Bean

Tripwatch Overlay:
a Book About Prayer

by Refried Bean

copyright 2016 by Refried Bean
distributed by Smashwords, Inc.

this book is for people
who want to pray more,
or less, or differently,
or at all.

The Lord's Prayer (Matthew 6:9-15)

"This, then, is how you should pray:
'Our Father in heaven,hallowed be your name,
your kingdom come,your will be done,
on earth as it is in heaven.
Give us today our daily bread.
And forgive us our debts,
as we also have forgiven our debtors.
And lead us not into temptation,
but deliver us from the evil one'"

July 17, 2016

Hi everyone, it is Sunday, July 17. It is National Ice Cream Day, and yesterday was National Guinea Pig Appreciation Day. On both of these days I visited a place called the Cloisters right next to my neighborhood in Northern Manhattan. It is an art museum that is made up of four old French monasteries that got shipped to New York from across the ocean. It is on the top of a hill surrounded by a park that overlooks the Hudson River. The richest guy ever, named John D. Rockefeller, supplied the money for the museum to be created. It is full of medieval art, and a lot of it is Christian art.

I did not visit the Cloisters for a long time because I was worried that the art would hurt me. I have trouble viewing unwanted images because I have been shamed so much from forced exposure to obscenity and the humiliation from having my mind read as I interpret messages in a culture where people say all kinds of nasty stuff all the time. But it turned out that I love the art at the Cloisters, and I am so happy that they included a broader range than just religious art. There are tapestries with Unicorns and a deck of playing cards from the 1400s.

Anyway, that is a little background information, but what I am trying to say is that I have thought several times about how I need to write a book about prayer and share all my best ideas for praying, because I have learned a lot about prayer and I want for other people to be able to cash in as much as they can, and I especially want them to have the blessing of knowing that other people in their lives and in their thoughts will also probably get all kinds of blessings as they pray.

Being at the Cloisters museum inspired me, and I think I will go ahead and write this book, and write it in a journal format that I can work on as I keep visiting the Cloisters. One of my prayer ideas I sometimes use is to ask God to reapply other people's prayers to new populations, and being in courtyards surrounded by monasteries where people prayed full-time is a way for me to remember all kinds of prayer power and potential.

So I am starting my book today.

I think it would be good for me to say early on in this book that I often pray the Lord's prayer that is listed in the book of Matthew when Jesus teaches his disciples how to pray. They ask him how to pray and he tells them a specific prayer that they can say and of course I am sure it is good to really mean it. I say that prayer every time I climb the three flights of stairs to my apartment, and I pray it often at other times, too. One thing I really like to do is to think of a category of people, or several categories, and include as many people as possible, and then I pray that prayer for a lot of people at once. I think it is a way of caring enough to pray for specific people, but it can apply to a huge group of people and maybe even have indefinite boundaries so more and more people keep being blessed, forgiven, saved, fed, and comforted. It takes time to memorize that prayer and use it as a habit, so take your time and do not feel despair if for a while or even years you can only remember a few lines or ideas from it.

That is not all there is to praying the Lord's prayer, even for me personally, but I wanted to mention this early in the book so that people would know that all of my other ideas are just part of a bigger picture and that some of their effectiveness may be because of this foundation that matches God's direct teaching in an indisputable way.

I am not going to take the trouble to defend every other idea by pointing out how it matches a sentiment or a request in the Lord's prayer, but I will say now that Jesus Christ told us to ask for daily food and maybe to ask for food every day, and there is a lot of stuff that can count as food, and there are a lot of activities and efforts in life that yield food of all sorts.

Jesus also said in the Bible more than once to ask God for what we want, to ask him for a lot, possibly to ask repetitively, and to just ask and ask and ask and have faith. So basically what I do is just keep asking God as much as I can for anything I can think of that anyone would want and I keep asking God to bless everyone and I ask him to help anyone I can think of, and I try to think of as many specific blessings for as many people as I can and I just order in bulk okay. That is what I do. I order in bulk, sometimes using actual pen and paper and charts.

There are currently 7 billion people in the world. There are also millions who have already lived and where are they? And wouldn't they like for their descendants and for all the rest of the generations to be okay. People need food every day. People need love and hope. And people every day are trying to do good and to survive which, more than people realize, requires all kinds of resources.

So this is one of my reasons for just brainstorming the biggest prayers I can think of. Some people might think a big prayer is one with big words and maybe some kind of thoughtful, considerate, complicated request for something to happen in someone's life. Really, that could be nice for people, but I am not a soap opera writer, and to me it seems like a bigger prayer is a prayer where you ask God to provide 4 billion ice cold lemonades, maybe for people on earth, and maybe for people elsewhere. It takes five seconds, and then you can move on to the next prayer or the next game of Candy Crush or Angry Birds. People might say that's flippant, but really, when you try to pray sincerely for other people's benefit (and your own!) you get to know God better and can securely pray what you would really want for people.

This sincerity issue is something that for me is another reason that the idea of praying in a bulk order format can be helpful. It becomes a job of sorts, and while you will really get to know God well while trying to think about whether each prayer is a reasonable request, in a way you don't have to struggle as much with motives because it is basically already established that you are just a servant doing a job which is the simple task of generating requests that match maximum supplies to maximum populations. I will say more about this, and whether people want to mix this idea with other options, like praying more for desired storylines in the lives of friends and family, is up to each person. People have all sorts of prayer gifts and I have heard people pray in the most wonderful ways that are different from my personal strategy. But my strategy is nice, too, because you don't have to know a lot of Christian concepts, or understand all the Bible stories and verses, and figure out what you think must be the will of God for everyone you know. Instead you just ask God for all the blessings you can think of for all the people you can think of.

I have two more main things to say as soon as I can in this book. The first one has to do with any kinds of feelings like why would God answer a prayer from me, and who am I to ask God for 40 billion factory days without injuries, or medicine for everyone, or candy for the poor children. I think that people write whole books on this issue, and the main thing I have to say is to pray for forgiveness for yourself as you pray, and if you sense that there is some reason that God would not accept your prayer, then make that thing right if you can. And if you can't, then probably you just need to pray and have faith and keep praying for people as much as you can. There is more to say but the main thing to say is pray anyway. Because if there are bad feelings it probably means something evil doesn't want people to have ice cream.

The other thing I wanted to hurry and say is also related to the issue of worrying about why God would want to hear from you, or doubting that he wants to answer your prayers, or thinking that you are not eligible to pray because of too much sin or not enough knowledge about God, Jesus, and the Bible.

Well this is the thing I am most excited to say. Catholics ask saints in heaven to pray for them all the time because those people were so good. And Protestants only ask Jesus and God because they say those saints aren't good enough to pray to or to ask for them to pray for us. But really, I think a wonderful discovery is that being on earth as a sinner might be the greatest prayer opportunity and time window that anyone ever has. It is now that we are in the middle of our own wrongs and the world's tangled up tricks and traps and evil and suffering, and we are the ones who know our friends and even our enemies, and we are the ones suffering from the cultural problems, and we are the ones with the bills to pay and the earth responsibilities, and we are in the mess, so we are the best located and in the best mindset to pray up the prayers that dissipate the evil haze or explode the structures of evil networks, or extinguish the fires of people's suffering. I mean you can take probably any analogy you could ever think of and it will probably turn out that it is not an analogy at all but something that literally happens every time you pray, and there are benefits probably from any prayer from any person and for any person, and the Holy spirit translates and improves prayer, too, I think. This is also something to keep in mind if you suffer with depression or need more reasons to live. I do not know everything, but I really believe that it is the people on earth who have a special prayer opportunity like no other. There has to be some kind of power and priority for people who are actually "on the ground." It is something to think about when deciding how much to retreat, too, and how much to be in a monastery, and what is the right mix of action and service and contemplation. I mean having some peace of mind or being in a peaceful location might mean you can pray more or better, but being persecuted in a horrific mess might mean that a couple of zaps saying God help us, help us God, God help us, might bring salvation to millions, which could be part of what happened on the cross, anyway.

Another good thing to keep in mind is that even the monks who spent their whole lives praying prayed a prayer that says, "Lord Jesus Christ, have mercy on me, a sinner," or maybe better yet, "Lord Jesus Christ, have mercy on us, we're sinners." Monks prayed this a lot, and who knows what people's sin situations are, I mean it is kind of ridiculous to think about really, but the fact is that there is a prayer to pray when you feel bad, and it is a prayer that you can pray for yourself and others. And I mean while you are at it why not throw in a request for some movie tickets or salvation for China.

Anyway, that is most of my ideas already said. That is all my secrets and logic, and my book isn't that entertaining so far, so really I think you have a lot to go on already if you don't feel like reading my other ideas.

That is enough for now, though I will mention one more thing, because there are some questions about repetitive prayer. King David in the Bible, who was truly great, told his son to keep his words few when praying. Ok so it is possible that God appreciates the person who says, "God, I know I never ask for anything, but will you heal so and so." You know there is actually a precedent for that. But Jesus Christ gave examples of people who pestered kings and would not give up until they got the bread they wanted, which to me is all the permission I need to keep on asking God for cash and prizes game show style for anyone who has ever lived or will live.

July 22, 2016

Hi everyone, today is Friday. I thought I would go back to the Cloisters this week and I haven't, but I still want to keep writing this book so I am going to go ahead and share a list of some of my prayer concepts that I might talk about. I wrote this list the other day. This is a list of some of the strategies I use to try to make as many requests for as many people as I can. You probably can understand some ideas just from looking at the words but there are others that I will have to explain more.

Concepts:

Population networks
Contagion
Hijacking
Recycling and meaning redemption
Distribution
Acknowledgement of knowledge, recognition of God as genius, things per things
Lists
Reapplication of other prayers
Rearrangement of already words
Advertising reach
Generation numbers
Leaving room for translation and improvement, almost complete prayers
Big mess plus lords prayer
Being in a crowd
Looking at a map
Choosing representatives
While you're at it prayers
Hundred hundred hundred
Reading for ideas
Optimal boredom situations
Keeping heaven in mind
Stress or walking boosts
Respectful hypotheticals
Actual charts and graphs
Sudden simplified
Supersizing other people's prayers
suspecting recognition that unlocks but then what unlocks then ask
Adopting cities or other populations
Going down actual lists of people or potential recipients
Teams and stadiums, points and winnings
Praying along to music using different words than the lyrics

Poetic Vision Contest
Expanding the Inclusion
Loose associations
Giving from your own personal stash
Praying for others with the same feelings or experiences of self or others
Triggers or designs on surfaces
Bonus rewards and multiplication instead of division
Images
3D grids
Photoshop
Praying for people in heaven and hell and on other planets
Jackpots
A-thons
Praying Against Evil
Prize package concept

Population networks

This is just a matter of choosing who to pray for and while you pray for one group that you think of, you can go ahead and think about anyone they might be linked with for any reason, like people who have seen the same commercial, or people who did the same good deed on a Wednesday afternoon. The idea is to pray for as many people as possible, and to include people who no one but God could ever predict that they would be prayed for at that moment.

Contagion

This is a similar concept, except it isn't just about choosing one time recipients, but it is about asking God to bestow some kind of blessing on people that causes anyone they interact with or have even been indirectly associated with to also get whatever set of blessings that you ask God to give them. So after you pray that prayer, the prayer keeps growing and more and more people keep getting blessed even after you have moved on in your mind. You can also ask for the blessing, like whatever designed set of blessings or forgiveness that you ask for, to keep growing in some way as more and more people get blessed.

Hijacking

This is when you take something that already exists, like existing communication or existing population networks, even if it has problems mixed in, and you capitalize on the work that has already been done in order to assign a prayer request to some people. There are many ways to do it, and simply praying for facebook friends is one way, but there are infinite possibilities. People could pray for everyone in a phone book or from a club, or do something like think of everything that has been stolen from children, put it all in one prize package, and then ask God to multiply it and give it to children and maybe to anyone who got tricked and donated money to a bad cause or to whoever is on some kind of school list or tax audit list or something. Then you ask God to give whatever blessings would fix the ratios and set right the reward system. That way everyone gets blessed, and if the actual requests include things like forgiveness and repentance and opportunities, then a lot of other things can happen to right the wrongs in what could be quite a mess reflected in a prayer that is also a mess. I mixed some different concepts in that example, but the basic gist of it is that you take anything you can think of that has already been done and attach prayers to the framework or network in a way that you think God would not mind answering. This is a category where approval and forgiveness is very important because you do not want to do offensive hijacks unless you acknowledge to God that it is offensive and that you are just wanting everyone to experience the extremes of His mercy.

Recycling and meaning redemption

By now you can see the similarities among some of these concepts, but this is another thing where something existing in some kind of ordinary or even disappointing format can be transformed into a request that could generate blessings for eternity. One example is taking a book or a library or a set of books or all the printings of a newspaper and ask God to remix the words to form a prayer that would bless ten thousand nations for ten thousand years and then ask him to restart an updated prayer every time the blessings phase has passed. A lot of time and effort gets wasted on earth, and this is a way to confess our foolishness on behalf of the whole guilty world, and to ask for redemption in a way that acknowledges that it is not something to be taken for granted.

Distribution

This isn't as much of a prayer concept as much as it is just a logistical necessity of praying and a multifaceted consideration of how the blessings will get distributed, how much, and in what way. In your mind you can design calendars or a schedule over years or ages for people to get repeated bestowals of surprises or necessities, or you can designate the quantity of something desired for individuals or groups or categories, or you could even almost imagine some kind of condition or storyline or mechanism that triggers or provides the main distribution of whatever thing you or asking for, or whatever set of blessings is in a prayer. One thing you could do is ask God to give everyone ten generations from now four thousand happy lunches or fifty compliments for each time that someone in this generation or five thousand years before endured a social situation that required exhausting vigilance. Or maybe you imagine some kind of account in heaven represented by a complicated shelf of bottles and the bottles are filled with some yummy drink or magic sand as blessings accumulate, and the blessings could get distributed as that person does something that they are good at, or does something that is difficult for them or for someone else they do it for. Or you can get the angels and saints involved and ask them to distribute health kits of magic coins all over the physical locations people will walk through like in a video game.

Acknowledgement of knowledge, recognition of God as genius, things per things

This is something to do all along the way, and it is also the foundation for praying as big of prayers as you can in the first place. God knows everything and is constantly creative and has created a universe with billions of solar systems. So the extent that his genius can be counted on and recognized in prayers is something important to think about when asking him to help everyone. He has been called the "God who sees," so when you ask him to send friends and hope to all the kids who got hurt by a math test or to give the whole world some kind of public happiness based on a young person's perseverance to keep a part time job, or anything else that depends on God's infinite knowledge, many purposes are served, and you also get to know God better while praying the prayers.

Lists

This is so simple and basic. People make lists of prayer requests in Bible studies and churches all the time, and why not just make a list and give that to God directly. It is kind of like in the movie Mary Poppins when they make a list of attributes for the nanny they want and then tear it up and throw it in the fire place and then Mary Poppins arrives with the list taped up and she is just like what they described. Also, lists can be matched. So you can take a list of names and match it with a list of blessings. Lists are also a way to do something active. So if you have trouble focusing when you pray, why not type a list of stuff you want. I mean who doesn't want to type a list of stuff that they want.

Reapplication of other prayers

This is one of my favorites, because I know that a lot of people pray better than me, and pray in different ways, and have friends with difficult situations that cause them to think of very thoughtful prayers. So you simply ask God to take all the prayers from certain people, or from a school, or from a church or a grocery store, and you ask them to be reapplied to a new population. I also like this because maybe some day those people who prayed so faithfully and secretly in certain ways will get a little bit of extra impact from their prayer, and maybe a little extra appreciation from everyone who benefited.

Rearrangement of already words

Ok this is the same thing as the words of a book rearranged by God as a prayer but you could also say okay maybe there are saints in heaven who would like a writing prompt or a prayer contest and they can take a few mysteries or sci fi novels from the library and rearrange words to write up some kind of wonderful blessing that then gets assigned to a group of people who might not have ever been prayed for by anyone.

Advertising reach

This is kind of like hijacking, but it is a little more specific, because basically what you do is accept that many people are literally reaching millions with messages and products and services every day. So you just take that same communication and try to attach some prayer to it by asking God to bless the customers or employees of certain companies, or maybe attach some kind of magic surprise to an advertisement, and some day in heaven the people who took a flyer from some one on the street will get a barrel of special stones and games delivered to their vacation home.

Generation numbers

Ok everyone this is something I am still personally working on and I have learned a lot about how I can improve. Once you have some prayers that you have thought of or are working on, and the more the better, I think it is good to try to apply them to the next generations. Simply praying for all the people of the future in whatever way makes sense is a great idea, but all these other prayer concepts can form a pretty big network of prayers, and it seems efficient to somehow make the requests for all the people who will live their lifetimes in this world. So what is needed is numbers. I sometimes just try to start counting while thinking of the prayers I have prayed and ask God to bless those generations. But are generations that well defined? I am not sure they are, so it is difficult, and it is also hard to keep counting into the future. One option is to do something like hijacking, which is borrowing numbers from another context. I sometimes borrow numbers from people with Obsessive compulsive disorder who count when they are anxious, and I recently thought of an exciting option of thinking of those population explosion environmental videos where people estimate how many people will eventually be in the world. Other options might be to try to assign prayers to all the new and evolving designs of favorite products and packaging, or some kind of aspect of reality that is not likely to go away. And what if people have done that for us? Like what if someone a long time ago asked God to bless all the children fifty times per thunderstorm. So while storms come and people get scared, their blessings accounts might be increasing the whole time. You can also try to reach people (and animals) by imagining the world spinning and think in astronomical terms, or go country by country, or even literally draw timelines and lists. This is just a concept to think about and to think okay how can I pray for all the future generations of people in ways more specific than just saying "Please God help everyone who ever lives, etc." Statistics and math books or even business receipts might also be useful for borrowing numbers.

Leaving room for translation and improvement, almost complete prayers

Okay, in a way, all prayers are already like this, and God interprets and improves our prayers as we pray. But sometimes, especially when trying to use all these concepts and think of blessings for all the different people, it gets messy, and it is hard to even think through a complete blessing. It just gets complicated, or you might lose a train of thought. Sometimes on purpose I will make my prayers messier or less complete and ask God to do something even greater based on what He knew my intent was. Or you can even say okay here is a little idea or thought or prayer, and could there be a prayer contest in heaven where people crush me and make it seem like I never should have ever prayed because what they thought of was so much better. You can also kind of speculate about other messes and then sort of present messes to God and be like Okay God, please help us and make something good come from this, and it can be as much based on prayer or circumstances as you and/or God decides.

Big mess plus lords prayer

Okay this is the exact same as the previous concept, but basically you think of others until there is a big mess in your mind, or you just think of a terrible mess on earth, and then you pray the Lord's prayer with those things in mind. It can be done based on location, based on shared experiences, based on history, or the desired ideal, or anything you can think of. I think that is one of the reasons that God gave us the Lord's prayer, is because we just don't understand what is going on and it is great to have some idea of God's values and will that always can apply.

Being in a crowd

I really think God likes this, and Jesus spent times in crowds and by himself. Something about being in a stadium or at a busy street festival can help people pray for strangers in a way that is very personal and probably has some great power because of proximity. I mean this is reason to consider moving somewhere specific to pray for people, like a big city, or your favorite country that doesn't have much church, or to walk an exercise route that passes a school, or to maybe go ahead and go to some concerts. People might not expect to be prayed for at all, but then you pray for them, and five years later they have some peace of mind or protection in a bad situation that has nothing to do with the crowd you were in. Probably you can also pray retroactively for crowds that you have been in or near.

Looking at a map

This is another pretty simple concept and with the great zoom in features on smart phones and computers, it can be pretty easy to spend some time looking at maps, thinking of countries, and praying for people that you might not have thought of before. It is a great opportunity, and seeing maps on a regular basis can help you keep more of the world in mind at all times. I think another good thing about it is the way you can use your elementary or middle school knowledge in a way that makes the most of the blessing of education and the geographical and news knowledge that not everyone in the world has always had.

November 16, 2016

A little break from the concept list

Ok everyone, I just filled in explanations for a lot of the concepts I listed but I am a little bit tired and thought maybe I will take a break from explaining all that and readers can have a break too. I think that there is definitely a pattern to the concepts and people can probably see the main ideas behind all of it. I think that this list can help everyone pray more for strangers and more and more people can receive unexpected help from God that they would never have even thought to ask for. It is good I think for some blessings from God to be expected, and to be factored in as a way of life, and for other help to be hidden until some surprising moment, when it turns out that God had some kind of support or surprise that no one would have guessed, and that nothing evil could ever have planned for or succeeded in destroying.

A few more thoughts

Yesterday and this morning I had insurance problems on my mind, and that is one of the trappings of life that became an ongoing burden for me and affected many choices and lack of choices about what I could do for people and where I could go for many years. But some of these restraints have put me on a path where I worked twelve years in a bookstore and now just finished social work school. The social work school I went to specializes in helping "populations," and there is a great emphasis on understanding the needs of marginalized groups. I did not choose the school based on the helpful way it matches my prayer life, or the ways that so many students, teachers, and clients can be links to entire populations of people who need any kinds of prayers anyone could think of. But it was a great match and a great way to add depth to my prayers while reaching more people who might have not been included in some of my other prayers. The unplanned perfection of this match also shocks me in a way and reminds me that these prayers I have prayed will probably be answered. I hope other people will feel hopeful about this, too, and take the time to pray for the people who they care about, because it is not a joke to move to a big city, to ask God for 10 million castles in heaven, and then to see a very obvious providence not just behind all of it but permeating the whole urban conglomeration of experiences, and of life and chores and work and food.

OK, back to the list:

Choosing representatives

This is just a concept and not necessarily a specific type of prayer. Basically the idea is that whenever anyone needs prayer, even though everyone is unique, there are probably hundreds more people who have a similar need and why not pray for all of them. Sometimes you can be the representative yourself, and if you are feeling heartbroken, you can pray for everyone who is heartbroken, or make that some kind of line and pray for everyone over that or experiencing less pain, etc. But I think really finding other people to be representatives is the most productive way to pray, and people can represent all kinds of groups or blessings. You can mix and match in all kinds of ways, and sometimes even ask God to mix people's company and blessings in various ways. I think that the sharing on social media is one way that God provides opportunities for blessings to be shared, and remembering what he has already done for people can be motivating. Sometimes I imagine visuals as well, and I might imagine a wave of blessings coming up behind someone that can wash over a whole group of people who need something, or who have something that can be shared with others.

While you're at it prayers

Okay this is a category that I think people who pray more normally might like. What I am thinking of as "normal" can actually be a very special discipline, and I don't mean to make it sound less valuable, but it is not something I am as good at as a lot of other people. But anyway I figured out that during the times someone has a major prayer request, it can be a good time to pray up as many other kinds of help that you can think of for them throughout their whole life and for their whole family and everyone they would be connected to in some way, even if it is people in photographs of their textbooks. The idea is that okay people are praying for their health or their heartbreak, but they have a whole life and why not pray for everyone and everything in that life while they are on your mind. This also helps with the way some things in life get a lot of care and support, and sometimes people go through stuff in a very lonely way because people do not understand when and how much people need prayer at other times.

Hundred hundred hundred

This is a specific kind of prayer idea that is a variation of the "leaving room for improvement" idea. This is something I do when I think of a really good category of recipient, or a great specific blessing, but I want the prayer to be bigger and bless more people. What happens is that my prayer becomes the theme for a bigger prayer, and I just say hundred hundred hundred hundred as many times as I can, and in doing that I am asking God to think of a hundred more categories of recipients, a hundred more categories of blessings, a hundred more methods of distributions or time periods, a hundred more types of contagion, and maybe even a hundred more concepts like "hundred hundred hundred." Often if there ends up being a loop like that, it is a good sign that the blessings can just keep going on and on, and maybe the prayer will eventually reach everyone who has ever lived. Does anyone find that cheesy or mockable? If you think feasts and healing are mockable then you have a problem but all these prayers are still for you and for everyone.

Reading for ideas

Ok I think that I thought of this one because of my attention span problems and anxiety disorder, but the concept is basically to pray the whole time while skimming a book or a catalog of some kind. You can choose any type of book you can, and you can skim it for prayer ideas and pray for anyone you can think of. It is also a good way of disguising your prayers, which is something that God likes. He likes for people to pray in secret and not to do everything for attention. Obviously I am writing a book and sharing my ideas, and I do have problems trying to get attention and admiration. But ultimately I have sincerity, too, and I will lose whatever rewards I need to share these ideas which I do think can help people love each other and help each other in neverending ways.

Optimal boredom situations

Ok here is another concept that isn't as much of a prayer content ideas as it is a description of a good prayer environment or a strategy for helping you be in a situation where you could pray more and better. I think everyone finds themselves in situations that are somewhat boring, and when you have a goal to pray for people, there can be optimum levels of boredom that cause you to pray while you pass the time, but where there is still enough mental stimulation or reminders of life that motivate you to think fast and well and keep praying. A part time or even full time job can be like this, or some time on the treadmill with the right TV station showing the news, or maybe the right pace of walking or jogging. Taking a good number of breaks or having some amount of social interaction during a several hour stretch of time that can be partially spent praying can also help.

Keeping heaven in mind

I really think this is the secret to all kinds of happiness and endurance, but it also is helpful for prayer, because if you keep heaven in mind, then you can literally pray for anything for anyone. And it is hard to know what can come true on earth and what really people would rather wait for and have permanently anyway. It can also allow for more creativity, like praying for magic coke machines. Creativity can squelch the boredom that makes it hard to keep praying, and it can also help you have hope for yourself and other people as everyone suffers in some way.

Keeping heaven in mind can also be a reminder of the reality that this life on earth is a one in a billion opportunity, but it is also a one in a billion blink out of eternity. So things can be important or not important in whichever way God most wants to bless us.

Stress or walking boosts

This is kind of the same concept as optimal boredom, but the idea is that there could be a certain kind of pressure that can boost the prayers or make you pray more fervently.

Respectful hypotheticals

Okay here's another crazy one. What if you take scenarios and say okay which people would have done such and such good thing if someone needed them to, and even though it didn't happen, ask God to give them an extra reward for what they would have done. Really it's pretty fun, and thinking of it can make you aware of how good a lot of the people you know really are in a lot of ways. Or use it to choose a category of recipients, like say okay who would have given up their subway seat, or who would have hired some of the other hypothetical winners, or who would win a music contest, and then ask God to give all of those people a bonus surprise every hundred years in heaven, plus some extra life on earth. Then if you add other concepts, like choosing representatives or contagion or big mess plus Lord's prayer, then before you know it there is a big blessing that started with something as simple as imagining a hypothetical situation.

Actual charts and graphs

This might be a little controversial to some people, and some people might find it disrespectful. I think a lot of people are really close to God in an emotional way and it seems flippant to make a list or a chart to help maximize the amount of requests presented to God. But I have found it helpful, and as I said before, it helps with my motives and my low self-esteem from sometimes not being successful in a worldly way. Jesus himself sometimes framed our relationship with God as that of a servant with a master, and I have found it to be thrilling and rewarding to basically fill out order forms as my way of asking for God's will to be done "on earth as it is in heaven." If people feel tempted to let other people read their prayer work, then just destroy it afterwards, or erase things as you type.

Sudden simplified

I do not really remember what this one is but I am guessing that it is something like just asking God to provide love for people or healing or just zapping people with one word prayers as sudden requests for them.

Supersizing other people's prayers

I try not to meddle too much with other people's prayers except to ask God to multiply what they would have been praying for and to ask him to give those blessings to as many people as possible. Then I ask for God to also bless the people who don't pray that much or at all, and to find something in their life that can be transformed into some kind of blessing trigger like what a prayer would have done. All kinds of people have different strengths and ways that they use their gifts to reach out to people, and when I am taking a break from generating my own prayers, why not ask God for a turbo boost on other people's prayers, or some kind of capitalization of the potential in the lives of people who might be doing something else that God wants them to.

suspecting recognition that unlocks but then what unlocks then ask

This is kind of specific but I like this concept and it is kind of based on the idea of curses and blessings, and requirements for things to be reset and people to be blessable. I do not know what all the rules are, but sometimes I think of how maybe certain acts of faithfulness might unlock blessings for entire peoples and nations, so I think of as many scenarios like that as I can, and then I simply ask for the special thing to happen, and for people to succeed, and for their prayers to be answered, and for God's forgiveness to help people be reconciled and blessable. I think I am getting into a theological mess now because the cross was so important in this way, but to me it seems like there a lot of situations where something crucial needs to happen, and why not pray for people not to be blocked from all the great things God can give them.

Adopting cities or other populations

Sometimes people pray continually for a certain country or city, or they just pray very faithfully for their own church, but there might be other groups worth adopting in that same way, whether it is a category of people who have something in common, or a group that actually knows each other. I sometimes like to pick people from historical periods a long time ago and then pray for their descendants, whether that is biological or something like philosophical. You can also sometimes pray for the inverse of those populations, like the people absent from that scene.

Going down actual lists of people or potential recipients

I think a lot of people do this or aspire to do this, but one strategy is to already maybe think of a set of blessings and then choose a phrase like "please give this to _____" and then repeat that while listing out names. You can do this silently at graduations, too and the challenge of not skipping anyone can be what keeps the tedium from preventing you from praying the whole list. If there are people who can have community without being hypocritical and doing everything for their own attention, splitting up a list with others in person can be an option. But I will say that I personally believe that there can be problems sometimes where an "us and them" mentality is destined to win out when people conspire over a "list of the lost."

But praying down lists can be great, especially for strangers that you wont meet and accidentally look down on because they were just a prop in your scene as you bonded with the in crowd.

I am being a little bit dark and cynical in a way and I don't mean to be.

Maybe I will balance that cautiousness with suggesting an extreme of just stacking a dictionary on a phone book and asking God to help everyone, bless them, and heal them and all the people who aren't on the list.

Teams and stadiums, points and winnings

This seems stupid, but wouldn't it be fun to get 45 million blessings per point that your favorite sports team wins? Well I don't think a prayer like that would offend God, though it might be good to thank him for just the sports fun by itself, too.

Praying along to music using different words than the lyrics

It embarrasses me so much when I think people know I am doing this, because it affects me as if I were singing a solo or something, but I have found that I can pray for longer if I am praying along to a melody, and it doesn't always matter that much what the words to the song are, though that can help too. It is very simple. A lot of people probably already do it, but I think more people probably sing along to worship songs instead. But why not add your own overlapping words where you pray for specific people and ask God for specific blessings. I am talking about singing silently of course.

Poetic Vision Contest

This could be done with a friend, and the competition is in the creativity more than in a way of trying to seem "good" in a bad way, but what if you think of some kind of hopeful vision of the future or the present where people have food, or hope and love crush the forces of darkness, etc, and then make sure those visions become requests for the best things you can think of to come true in the lives of whole societies.

When I taught high school, there was a suggested unit about the so-called "American Dream," which is commonly known as a somewhat individualistic dream of having a house and a family, and okay a car, and okay it often becomes very much about the stuff. And then that dream gets outdone in certain ways by people like Martin Luther King Jr. who have a bigger and maybe more noble dream. But really a lot of people have a bigger dream that involves the well being of a lot of people, including people who are not yet born. And what I am saying is that it could be good to kind of think about that, and go ahead and let that bigger dream "materialize" in your mind and turn it into a prayer.

Another related reference is part of the story of John the Baptist in the Bible, who eventually got his head chopped off, and he was asking someone to ask Jesus something, and Jesus said something like "Tell him the blind see and the lame walk."

Expanding the Inclusion

Ok this is a very simple concept to keep in mind, and the idea is to try to increase the amount of people prayed for in each individual prayer, especially when you have prayed well for someone. It can be done in all kinds of ways, and with all kinds of add on specifiers, like saying please give 45 million jackpots to all the Wal-Mart customers today, and all the people who did not go to Wal Mart, ok wait that's everyone except employees, okay so that's messed up so you just try to add to the prayer, then add Target customers, then people who don't have enough money to shop, or people who live in other countries, and descendents of Wal Mart Employees, or people who are wearing the same socks as people who are at Wal Mart right now... plus everyone who works in the factories where the Wal Mart products are made, plus hundred hundred hundred. Ok I think you can see the idea. And people say ok then why bother choosing a population or set of recipients at all, but it does make sense to choose people and have starting places, and this could be the greatest strategy to pray for people who everyone and the devil thought must be goners. But no, they chose the argyle socks this morning, plus God cares about them.

Loose associations

This is kind of a tactic and kind of just a concept that can be used when you are resting. I mean just pray a little bit casually, and whatever comes to mind can be a link for a more deliberate request, and then just keep going as long as you can, with plenty of rest in the mix, too.

Giving from your own personal stash

Jesus said to store up treasure in heaven so I think we must have some kind of stash of blessings there that is hopefully growing as we do what we are supposed to with true priorities. There is also God's infinite riches that is probably somehow behind any account we would have, so I try to dip into all accounts when praying, and I cash out stuff in heaven and ask God to give people blessings from whatever I have. Sometimes I clear out the whole account and start over. I have done it for many strangers and I did mean it. It is possible I over estimate what I had to give but heaven is going to be pretty great. I think that giving from your own blessings is a way of expressing personal appreciation, though I think usually if God gives us any blessings, some might be especially for us, and He seems happy to give from his own infinite kindness and creative, thoughtful blessings and astronomical resources. If you want to do personal gifts, then I think actual giving in your life like cash and food for people is important if possible, but God might really understand if praying is sometimes the best you can do. One other funny thought is that sometimes I try to take things from other people's heaven accounts just as a joke or as a fun surprise if I think they wouldn't mind. I don't think that cashing out blessings for earth is to be done too lightly, but when people suffer, it does make sense to try to borrow from heaven.

Praying for others with the same feelings or experiences of self or others

I have kind of already mentioned this but I want to mention it again in a very serious way. Most of us hear about a lot of problems every day, and sometimes in work situations or geographic locations you become aware of all kinds of specific suffering. Letting this suffering be on your mind and praying for all people with each problem that you hear about is one of the best ways that I have found to pray sincerely. The realness of people's pain and heartbreak usually makes any hypocrisy on your own part as a praying person dissolve completely as you would do almost anything to ease their suffering. This kind of prayer can really affect someone's mood and heart, so it could be a situation where people need to occasionally count the cost and be careful with how depressed or sad they let themselves get. However, it also seems very related to the grief of Christ, and whatever reasons made people call him the "Man of Sorrows," and I think it can be well balanced with all the whimsical tricks that I am suggesting to ask for as much help and as many blessings as possible.

Triggers or designs on surfaces

This is something fun to imagine, like designing a color coded key of blessings and then assigning it to different patterns like wallpaper or other designs in people's lives. Then if they are near the pattern then hopefully the blessings get applied to them. So as people go about their daily business, everyone is getting blessed and protected from Satan. I think part of the idea is one of the most important concepts related to the acknowledgement of God's infinite knowledge. To try to design a complicated blessing like that not only is a way of depending on God's character and skill and genius, but it is also something that it seems impossible for evil forces to interfere with. I mean are the demons going to try to lead people away from wallpaper? It is absurd, and how could anyone or anything stupid enough to be evil in God's face ever suspect a strategy like that, much less steal the blessings prepared by an all powerful good God.

Bonus rewards and multiplication instead of division

Ok this is a concept that has to do with God's unlimited supplies. There are a lot of different ways that it can affect prayer, but the idea is to ask God to multiply and duplicate blessings when you start thinking of more people to pray for, instead of dividing a limited amount of blessings. Like if you want to personally ask God to reward someone who did something nice in front of you or for you, you might ask God to give them ten million blessings, and then give everyone else in their city the exact same set of ten million blessings. I mean why couldn't he copy a reward and give it to everyone. And then maybe that person will get a little extra bonus for doing whatever they did. People think okay now this is getting a little crazy because who am I to judge. Well who is anyone to pray and yet God sent his son to teach us how, even while being crucified on a cross.

Images

Some people pray more visually anyway but I think that images and analogies can be used when thinking of requests for God to help people. I mentioned a wave image earlier, but I have also borrowed images from movies, like certain kingdoms and scenery from Star Wars scenes, or concepts like Frodo destroying the ring in the Lord of the Rings stories, or cartoon images of libraries. The image of bottles full of colored liquids representing accounts was an image inspired by a movie image, and I also sometimes think of things myself, like some kind of grid of metal flaps that flip a different way after a prayer is prayed, and then water or something like that flows in a different direction. I think some people are even more image oriented than that, and they might be able to use that in a creative way to pray for people.

3D grids

This concept is kind of like asking God to send little angel bugs to tag people with blessings for now or later, but the specific idea is kind of like a game show and you just ask for there to be an invisible 3D grid filling up a whole store or building or location, and within each invisible box, there is some kind of prize people win if they walk through that grid. And as people win the prizes, the ones that are higher up come down kind of like in the Tetris video game, and more people can win all the prizes. Blessings can be distributed later on in ways that might also provide people with some recognition, or they can be given by God in secret ways where no one ever knows about the prayer or the person walking through the grid. You can also use 2D grids and ask God to make the floor tiles be filled with winnable prizes.

Photoshop

It is weird that a computer program would become a whole category of prayer ideas, but a lot of the design concepts, like running an image through a filter that gives it a watercolor look to it, or selecting the inverse of a shape, or flood filling colors, or simply designating blessings for each color in a scene are all ideas that can be used while praying for people. It is another way of thinking visually when praying and not just praying storylines for people, or praying with lists of nouns, like I like to do. But those things can also be combined with the Photoshop ideas.

Praying for people in heaven and hell and on other planets

We have plenty of people to pray for on earth, but a lot of people have already lived, and when Jesus died on the cross and then rose from the dead, he brought a lot of people back from the grave with him. It is something that doesn't get mentioned that much. I don't know what all is going on in other places, so I pray for anyone I can think of. And I can think of surprises that people in heaven might like, like a surprise cheese plate for my patron saint, and I can think of a lot of relief that God might be willing to give someone in hell if a person on earth took the time to pray for it. And who knows what kind of intergalactic battles are going on, or blessings that creatures on other planets might enjoy. So I just want to say yeah I pray for a lot of people, even knowing that this time on earth is the opportunity of the day, and I am here with the people I am with for a reason.

Jackpots

I have mentioned reapplying people's prayers, which is similar to this concept, which has more to do with taking all of the actual blessings that people have asked for and putting them into one jackpot and then asking God to give people that jackpot. I like to do it with buildings, like making a jackpot with all the prayers prayed for by the people who have been in a certain building, but I mean you could go pretty crazy and do a whole country or even all of Christendom or something and make that a jackpot and then ask God to give that to people from another building or country. And there is all of eternity for people to get the blessings, so why not pray a prayer as big as you can. You can also jackpot your own prayers, and if you go even a week trying to ask God to give everyone you know 45 million blessings each, then the jackpot gets exciting pretty fast.

A-thons

This is another concept that has multiple purposes. The idea is to take something repetitive people do, usually tedious, and then ask for that amount of blessings to give to them or other people. Like such and such blessings per unit of work or endurance. So if people in a store have to scan a lot of merchandise or if someone has to wash a lot of dishes, or some other pattern, then you say something like God please give such and such elementary school kids or such and such fast food workers 40 million jackpots for each time that the factory people find an unsellable item. This is one of my favorite ways of trying to help people benefit more from some of the things in life that can seem either futile or just not fun. I really think God does this anyway and has rewards already planned for everyone. But if you actually pray up some blessings based on some recognition of people's experiences, it helps you remember God's promises of reward and redemption, and it also helps you appreciate people's efforts more in this life.

Praying Against Evil

I just want to say in this book that I do ask God to bring death, shame, and annihilation to child abusers and bad people who truly ruin the world. I still ask God for all kinds of forgiveness for pretty much everyone, but after a certain point, I believe that riddance and justice become the first priority, and prayers should reflect that. I don't just leave that messy stuff up to the cops and the angels. I let myself care about crime victims and even just the every day victims of bad policy and abuse of power, and I beg God to destroy the people who put nasty images in our faces, who stare at women who aren't theirs to stare at, who tax people unfairly and misuse money they had no right to spend, who block people's good and reasonable goals with all kinds of emotional or physical tolls, and who charge too much for things like medical care or food for hungry children. Some of my rage is from personal experience, so I am extra careful to ask God for as much forgiveness as possible, maybe after people die, but I definitely ragefully ask God to crush the evil forces, and... the bad people, which do exist, and do hurt people every day.

Prize package concept

I think this is the main concept I use, which is listing out blessings in a prize package so it is easier to pray up a whole huge list of blessings when I see people or think of groups that I want to pray quickly for. Here is a copy of the main prize package I use, which is Prize package 63. This prize package is featured in my novel, along with some of my other prayer ideas. As of the writing of this book, I am currently working on Prize Package 89 and adding to it as much as I can when I think of blessings for people. Some of the phrases in this prize package sound random, but they are not, though I think random word generation could be used by God and translated to mean the most wonderful surprises anyone could ever want.

Prize package 63

grace
love
peace
joy
forgiveness
hope
health
wealth
understanding
wisdom
jokes
friendship
unexpected reunions
shelter
chocolate
opportunities to serve
self-actualization
Prize packages 1-62

protection from evil
intervention
help from angels
more love
power
family blessings
decency
smooth sailing
adventure
mercy
talent
virtue
recognition for a job well done
helpful environments
resources
art
good habits
supplemental bonuses
supersized prayers
good grades
a mentor
justice
victory
excellence
surprises
extra attention from the Holy Spirit
good leadership
mental health
inspiration
extra help
extra teaching
inclusion
discernment
kindness
Waffle House meals
permanent things

candy
church
reward
action
riddance of harrassers
recipes
expected and unexpected gifts, blessings, and help
contribution
early stuff
overlapping blessings
results
resistance
exemption
preparation
compensation
water
nourishment
trips to the mountains
fresh air
gentle correction
nourishment
contentment
doritos
just the right movie at just the right time
perseverance
diligence
morsels
good prayer life
worn paths and habits of love
deliverance
meaningful work
effectiveness
strength and will to spend time wisely
intelligence
gratitude
gentleness

goodness
self control
social skills
animal prize packages and prize packages for animals
literacy
healing
contentment
toys and games
stability
firepit fun and s'mores
glimpses of forever
good chairs
a special watch
good parenting
repair
the benefit of the doubt
beach and mountain fun
balance
entertainment
good company
employment
gear and equipment
opportunity to fix mistakes
something to be good at
support
understanding from others
understanding for others
knowledge
glory
45 million miracles
obvious answers to prayer
confirmation of favor and help
progress
treats
tolerance and intolerance
safety

social courage
immortality
minimized frustration
ancient blessing restarts
privacy and publicity
kindred spirits
good times with children
love from superiors
chance to mentor others
compassion for others
compassion from others
productivity
self-esteem
growth
maturity
creativity
45,000 surprises
happiness
medicine
reassurance
repeat blessings
good environments
good attitudes
perspective
good harvests
graduation
good stewardship
good speech
words of life
   low stakes when they mess up, high stakes when they do something right
   a swarm of invisible angel bugs that go around kissing them and all the people around
   them and whoever gets kissed by an invisible angel bug gets 45 million prize
   package 63s and other secret blessings

everything in Lord's prayer
everything in Psalm 23

special talent and opportunity to use it for benefit of others

special dinners out

special dinners in

ability to heal others

inspirational movie at just the right time

humor

comedy

laughter

improvement

Christmas

ice cream for the world

having nice things said about them

good reports

something for their troubles

visits from therapy dogs

time and will to read about others

time outdoors

chance to win something

second chances

redemption

motivation

good moments

good timing

secret food

strength to break bad habits

relationship blessings

care from loved ones

protection from despair

motivation to serve

transportation

things to share

good time at a festival

day trips
dog safety
special help at the end of life
mobility
privileges
supernatural hunches
wonder
awe
unexpected resources
people you can always count on
a bonus prize
spiritual growth
intellectual growth
career growth
social growth

inclusion

special friends

a whole bunch of moments in time when they are all that they wanted to be

freedom

100 different types of blessing contagion and contagious contagion so other people also get 45 million prize package 63s

truth
determination
contentment

courage

confidence

aerial views
rejoicing for others
magic glory

thrills
good changes
transportation
obedience

competence
pain relief
stress relief
other relief
immunity
strength
meaning
satisfaction
refreshment
technology
exercise
good smells
advantages
good temperament
catharsis
good parenting
safety nets
rest
relaxation
realizations in time
efficiency
effectiveness
abundant life
inheritance
skills
glowing work
wheels
tickets
music
pure motives
consideration for others
consideration from others
love that makes disappointments not matter as much
extra fun day off
special vacation

good sleep

inventions

callings

comraderie

promotion

treats

sincerity

45 million preventions

infinity prize packages designed by angels

opportunity

hope in a time of trouble

sanctification

good transitions

kind overrides

exposure of goodness

learning opportunities

helpful information

accident prevention

protection

contagious goodness

emotional support

good scenery

warmth

shelter

marketable skills

gravy

compliments

faithfulness

fear of God

attention span

life changing document

bargains

grief relief

ratios and infinity
help with math
sympathy and empathy
financial peace
cash
good thinking
appreciation
discernment
foresight
adaptability
harvest of righteousness
ambition
honesty
integrity
resolve
humility
a mystery and a joke
goods and goodies
intelligence
patience
corn blessings

wheat blessings

blue blessings

plastic blessings

edible blessings

intangible blessings

round blessings

square blessings

murky blessings
clear blessings
long blessings
short blessings
military blessings
airborne blessings
outdoor blessings

indoor blessings
furry blessings
tight blessings
loose blessings
paper blessings

cooperation
thoughtfulness (for and from)

chance to serve on a close knit team

good entertainment

self awareness

self-forgetfulness

Ohio blessings
diligence
creativity
innovation
problem solving skills
academic skills
strength
light blessings
dark blessings
permeable blessings
opaque blessings
multi-colored blessings
Biblical blessings I don't know to ask for
housing
permission
resources
backup
support
sponsorship
education
extra recess
birthday prize packages
ability to trust in God
knowledge of God

passion
books
good walks
honest work
what they really want
time
fun
good pets
fair food
being good at basketball
immunity
innocence
entertainment
skills
party cheese
extra things to look forward to
restoration
rejuvenation
refreshment
thoughtfulness
special fabric
meaning
purpose
goodness
greatness
good transportation
supernatural hunches
prevention of recurring nightmares and horrific realizations
accurate perception of reality
recovery
strength
friendship with people from other culturesand backgrounds
bright futures
success
marzipan
more grace

more love
more faith
more peace
hot blessings
cold blessings
liquid blessings
sifted blessings
forgiveness
regret prevention
obedience
light
gifts
flavor
shade
advancement
mastery
good thought and prayer lives
popularity
pay raises
promotions
reminders
snack day 99
someone to tell
deception prevention
clothes
snacks for angels
sanity
forcefields and safety walls
companionship
endurance
healing
beauty
44,000 victories
capacity and willingness to forgive
wooden blessings
fun trip with friends

fun trip with family
restoration
fun times in the dark
fun times in the light
credibility
oatmeal
rescue
sobriety
something for their trouble
fashion courage
satisfaction
bacon
immunity
surprise dessert
discipline
blankets
homefulness
accomodations
confidence
reconciliation
restoration
contentment
revelations
access
endurance
reason and logic
a secret chair
a surprise chair
delight
camp
miracle food
crispy blessings
good soup
good bread
success at four extra things
medical care

good advice
magic groups
commitment
improvement
animal blessings
adventure
good thinking
skills
salvation
happiness
dedication
perseverance
certainty
security
participation
completion
comfort
guidance
strength to accomplish goals
a time when their favorite sports team beats everyone
attention
productivity
awareness
taffy
insight
solutions
innovation
coordination
goodness
lunch money
reserves
art therapy
science jackpots
backups
faith
rest

prize package 359
a superior who notices them and looks out for them
safety in storms
friendship with God
good worship
dental health
consistency
pleasure
composure, wisdom, and safety during crisis situations
prevention of crisis situations
help dealing with disappointment
help overcoming weaknesses
realistic expectations
priorities in order
stuff anyway

opportunities to win, strive, and achieve
vision care
45 million jackpots
45 million grand prizes
45 million super bonus ultra sonic prize package 44s
45 million better yets and beyond thats
45 million everythings
45 million loop set extravaganzas
45 million maximum zaps plus double category zaps (exponential and contagious)
45 million gridathons, supergridathons, and supragridathons
45 million things not ruined
45 million all-inclusive complex linked spectrum pattern beam prizes plus bonus loops
magnetic contagion distribution
mega chop surplus divvies
backpack numbers category-selection-pattern-trigger-inclusions
roars and rumbles
frontier booster prize advances
cartoon concept representation jackpots
3D building gridalations

    tailored multiplying concept extension eternal loops and nonloops
    interpretation variation expansion application coupons plus copy ticketer
    linkbursts
    alignment
    space fame
    a camel
    simple things
    night club monastery link bonus account all-inclusive refill triggers honor theme 1000 plus 1000 exponent association perpetual research/nonresearch stat match contagion plus high range with background number pattern prize package jackpot sequences
    second chances
    third chances
    get out of jail free cards
    deliverance from evil
    extra Psalm 23 blessings
    Ezekiel blessings
    vision
    invitations
    hope
    traction
    the works hundred hundred eternalized
    curse-a-thon benefit receive-gives
    zap train mingle frees
    the bother-me line shuffle for everyone everywhere
    good day lane activations
    comedy angel dispatches
    step-guard infomercial translation exacto-matches
    good music
    direction
    freedom from sin
    improvement
    perfect way to serve in church
    change of scenery

time with loved ones
friendship
discipline
freedom from addiction
lemonade
healing
ideas
jokes galore for children
jokes galore for everyone
extra credit
successful attempts at blowing up death stars
supplies
harmony
eligibility
a good exit
purple drink that makes you feel good
restoration
transformation
renewal of the mind
intellectual stimulation
satisfaction
fulfillment
tears of joy
tears of healing
emotional health
career opportunities
laughter
gratitude
the right mix
participation
stacking block zaps plus map overlay irreversibles
Mary Poppins multi-rent snaps
graph translation contest result group distributions
generation skip reverse uno pattern prize sequence surprise loop all-includes
heaven prayer contest club beneficiary membership

rescue and riddance permanent justice combos
escape from personal hells
curse jar trick-and-traps
scale overlays
nonathons
footstep activation jackpots
sibling extension cash-in extravaganzas
age range 100 variation meaningless perception remix all possibility repetition zaps
zap decoy delay adds
tree-heals
endless reason-based speed paced bonus adds plus unlimited all-includes
multi-level variety growth strategy map selection sessions with factor increase quad code
math-a-thon increased unsuspect monitor result cash-ins plus unsuspect live wire portals
the right words for others
the right words from others
inspiration to achieve
inspiration to love
reminders of people in need
more wisdom
committee of saints in heaven praying for them and everyone in their life
energy
information
deliverance from evil
pain prevention
mistake prevention
technological blessings
protection from harm and harmers
immunity
survival
provision
favor

abundant life
good digestion
friendship
risk threat translation wage multipliers plus infinity bonus spec 1000s
infinity blessing decoy chain literally for every single thing
screen saver savers
retroactive wild card designations
type 10 initial assortments
freeze frame select spiffs
generation chore-a-thon all something
defense
art and music
holiday happiness
enough and extra
inverse something
achievement
forcefield that makes blessings unstealable
good times with animals
golden speech golden hour highlight expo markup boards
unsaid remix list apps
schedule difference match transports something source something
good company
surprise money
good stewardship
three more wishes
salvation anyway coupons
friends

Gum brand distribution cakewalk alter stain neverend chain trigger complexing all world staff loop hundred art interpretation redo zap thousand expo need feed overdo webs plus line repeat space force and flood fill extra adds
Thread trail surprise
Tone meaning plinko shocks

    infrasomething ticketed seasonal light show with blessing
attachment expanding trigger-sequence shadow layers and realm 5
filter hundred base square assortment detectable-later-transcenders
    dog bath pattern underground city applications
    directory shuffles
    already source tap-ins
    retro team assemble gifts
    10,000 rare and specials
    absurd measures
    other thing
    best Christmas spotlight replications
    cleverness
    cures
    blockers and decoys
    retro-fool-proofs
    immunity
    disease prevention
    a suitcase full of money
    good ideas
    fractal patterns blessings and distribution
    comedy context transfer chart zap all adds
    translation expo concept machine shares
    later anti-deserve stumble-upons
    prayer contest theme starts plus assorted share patterns with
variety restarts
    a resounding yes in their hearts
    freedom
    wisdom
    boats
     a chance to see migrating birds
    the justice of their cause shining like the dawn
    perfection
    competence
    recovery
    the choicest
    ancient prayers for the future

gizmos and gadgets
originality
the James C. Peabody center for food, comfort, and healing
preparation
45 million jackpots
all of the blessings language can describe
all of the blessings language can't describe
the strength to give up these things

And in Heaven....

A giant gingerbread house without a child-eating witch
a movie about their earth life
membership in an elite secret society
inclusion in an inclusive nonsecret society
45 million scoops of goodies
20,000 coupons
a bag of magic marbles plus refills sometimes
aquarium restaurant
comedy school
two wheelbarrows of sparkling surprises from the surprise quarry
a 40 room treehouse with a trunk staircase that leads to a cave
passes to the magic orchard
space trips
castles
a Holodeck and a transporter
videos of hypothetical situations
a giant flying dog to ride around on
magic utensils that make food appear
50,000 extra secret party invitations
hoverboard
ocean tour
shipment of hoodies for their people
retroactive favorite things video reapfest

a muppet lunch box with candy and a magic pen and a magic notepad
weekly scoops of goodies
own personal star named after them
vacation planet
a cool looking bird that follows them around
purple blessings
yellow blessings
granulated blessings
grainy blessings
45,000 barrels of supplies
a library card for the library of biographies written by guardian angels
treasure delivered by a fleet of ships
supplies dropped from the air
magical spray
coupons for the buffet of all foods ever invented
vacation with admired historical figure
inclusion in the lazy river cave network
a mystery pet
a magic piano candy and juice dispenser
membership in the gift basket club
panel times
food club
present club
infinite decoy half surprise club plus membership expansions
a watch with a button on it that makes there be an instant sno cone hut
a maze of bookshelves
a candy aisle maze
coins for the pinball arcades
trip to visit the real Santa Claus
dinner with favorite people from bible
supplemental bonuses
taste-tester club membership
a magic trampoline sky course

 citywide chocolate syrup system
 a huge wooden chest with drawers full of recipe cards for recipes only they know about
 a special variety orchard with underground tunnels connecting to the other special variety orchards
 999999999999999 dream jobs
 560 googly-eyed floopydoos
superpowers
an interesting machine
finding a suitcase full of money every now and then
45 million supersonic ultra mega jackpot prize packages
a trillion more prize package 63s
40 million maximums
infinity everythings
daily grid blessings
comedy prayer parlor sessions
party castles
booster button part time jobs
code 5 society
joke generation zone amps
best fest blessed rest
qualifier trail step plus portal option
refill dish technology sales
deliver club surprise pass-on loop multiplier variety combo
later save no way layer
welcome list pixel codes
billion year complex earth symbol selection line match catch
pop quiz minstrel super supper bonus menu
flight code chore detail
creature corner wave desk
rate comp sky charge success
wall fix light lamps
port kit number multi meaning card wheels
the revisit leaf creature medley
metal relief hope line read bakes
the non space other say red wait

speaker chicken list loops
center station window word flight
R code result bases
rock life pulley all material preserver tools
the anything is everything store
product hope spins
orbit deal central
the factory wish guarantee
tree bank
the other day
junkyard post
the wisdom book light
zone retrospectives
vendor surplus time jump shipments
future samples
spectrum beams
course extravaganza watch
catalog clubs billion plus accumulation mix
eyelight
all earth mistake translate scatters
extra animals
check offs
assignment bonus
element play tickets
standard compartmental walls with alternating key punch wonderflippers
flight light shuffle snacks
kickalong snap rock clicker gridders
stripe pipes
pathstone light chips
sandzoom water path sign jumps
interpretation contest result replay triggers
the forgiveness flag
meaning filler marker turns
behaf count send wins
the harvest fire circle

    shield flare stone bowl days
    a plastic bag of arcade tokens and magic coins for each plastic bag conserved on earth
    a special couch. a magic couch.
    a book where the characters give you food
    swarms of invisible angel bugs
    swarms of visible angel bugs
    space travel extravaganza
    floopydoos around every corner
    everyone gets a barrel

November 20, 2016

Hi everyone. I have gone to the Cloisters a couple more times and mostly stayed outside. It is a nice little hike with a good view of a river and once I saw some raccoons near the paved path. Two days ago I went there to see a few friends but I didn't end up going in the building and looking for them. I think I am about to finish this book, though, so I am glad for one more Cloisters trip.

Today is National Absurdity Day. That might be some of the reason behind some of the insurance problems I am having. But absurdity can also be awesome and is one of my favorite literary tools and one of my favorite theological terms. One of the things listed in the prize package 63 is "an absurd measure," and that is something that I ask God for sometimes. It is a recognition of his extravagance and mercy, and a prayer that His blessings for the people I pray for would be just a little bit over the top and possibly inappropriate in a certain comical way. It is a prayer that Christmas would be every day, and that people would put their socks on and find that all their socks have been turned to Christmas stockings full of toys and candy. It is also a prayer asking that me and everyone would be capable of forgiving in a way that creates that measure in our lives. Jesus said that the measure you get in life or maybe later will be the measure you use. That is one of his mysterious combinations of justice and mercy, and he is telling us that we have a say in the matter. I think some people who are a little more strict and expect greatness or even demand it from people in their society might have a great thing going on with the measure they use and the measure they get from God, but I really like to imagine something absurdly generous and absurdly forgiving. I have not been able to maintain this vision very well sometimes, and I have anger problems that make me pray for people to get in trouble sometimes. But I still try to forgive as much as I can, and to give as much as I can, and I think that being like Pig Pen from the Peanuts is going to make Judgement Day interesting. I mean it could take several days to sort out my mess of grudges and gifts.

But anyway, what I am saying is that the gift of Christ was absurd in a certain way, and Christ himself also told everyone to ask for things and to give and forgive. And he has now been given all authority in heaven and earth. So to me, if someone who prayed that people would be forgiven while he was being tortured on the cross says to ask him for stuff, then I am going to ask for as much stuff as possible, and I am going to go ahead and hope for a ridiculous amount of surprises, definitely in heaven, and hopefully on earth. Bad things happen on earth, and people take stuff away, but even the worst things might be part of a process that results in the securing of some kind of wonderful thing only years away, and it is likely to be something too wonderful to guess and can never be taken away.

Maybe people already know all of this but I think that there might be a clearance rack that people aren't seeing, and a grand opening or store closing that people haven't heard about, and if we even say oh no I never pray and pray a prayer like "Please give everyone all the stuff for the prayers I didn't pray," there could be some kind of jackpot situation unlike anything that the world has ever seen except for all the other times every single day that God blesses us with sun and rain and food and jokes and candy and games and friendship and happiness and forgiveness and hope and love and healing.

And as for other failures in my own prayers or in my life that could probably have added more power to those prayers, I am comforted by the verses in the Bible that say people who have been forgiven much love much, and love covers a multitude of sins. I mean the way God has it set up is so rigged in our favor that we almost can't lose, and if we do, we might still win.

I would like to say something else about the weirdness of my prayers. I mean some of it is a little odd, and maybe a little nerdy, and sometimes kind of a reverence risk. But I think a lot of it evolved as I endured very difficult struggles with mental illness, and it is a special thing that I am still alive to pray at all. The hope and sometimes certainty that maybe one day one of my prayers, or even all of them, might help people in a happy way has been one of my reasons for living, and to me it is a worthy cause that makes up for almost anything else that the world has taken away, or that I have lost through failure. And I believe that for other people, too, and that God has the power to take any prayer and answer it in a way that makes it as powerful as ten million prayers from ten million saints and angels.

November 21, 2016

Today at my therapy appointment, my therapist told me that there is an elevator up to the Cloisters at the A train 190th street station. So I am very excited and hopeful about future visits and maybe more journaling. I think I am going to let this be all I say now, though, and I will finish with the beginning list from the Prize Package 89 that I am working on:

prize package 89

lemon desserts for everyone
stench transfers
Wubble million spectrum
candy
gigs
secret passageways
tentacle hologram protection capability
signs and wonders
disaster opposites etc.
nature translation
meaningless work translation
chocolate tasting
account boost lecture series
chicken dinner
the leftover impossible
milk
gourmet baskets
new shoes
the millennial coupon book
a discovered drawer
good noodle
slushies
50 thousand unlimited favorites
400 more songs

designated plan paths
prize package 63
prize package 55
prize package 41
the inverse jackpot assortment
the later choose panel access
channels
mechanical favor
dice
lamplight
pain relief
group attention
catalog spree
sauces plus atmosphere match
angel fire
a good name
surprise kind animal happiness
the cartoon corner
deluxe ripe pick
umbrella selection
skylight
toys and games
metal
the correct structure
wise people
the million favor interpretations
cookies
something extra to give
elevation
consideration
the ice cream bar card from candyland
junk store
good deals
charge success
food life love combos
the extra good plot

courses
happy match
friendship with God
the prayer and the strength at all the times plus extra
good character
winning and won
pizza and ice cream
the unknown prize packages
space council VIP status
500 randoms and 500 normals
the dictionary translation blessing sequence plus search yield solar pattern
blue plate blue light UFO oh my gosh
punch card dial out spin smilers
the magic yarn
whole theme thousand thousands
the special thought layered list eternalized
bad people busted and burning
fundamentals and foundations
paint
color
rocks
wood beams
frogs and turtles
arts and crafts
cheese grits
steak and eggs
warm handoffs
good phone calls
presents
satiation
coordination
continuation
loop riddles
company
kind words and faces

good drink
cannister rations plus eternal hike provision
peace of mind
video games
puddings and pies
custard
lakes
wire circuit time jump other worlds
plans
replacement letter communication enhancements
alphabet favor
getting through it
not being bothered
the old testament shuffle
bread
cake
conspiracy gifts
shout-outs
thread mix
protections and preventions
hats and scarfs
tripwatch overlay
burden relief
the gleaming central triumph
milkshakes and smoothies
appetizers
the books
guys we've got a code 5
another suitcase full of money

November 29, 2016

    I think I will go ahead and add one more thought about prayer here. It is a thought I had recently when reading a book about torture. Some people lose their faith entirely or say they don't have faith because of all the horrible things that happen in the world. And in a way it is not necessarily the most faithless thing to look at evil and think that it is Godless. Christians have a hymn that says "though the darkness hide thee," and maybe some spiritual doubt in horrible circumstances might really affirm the goodness of God and the way God doesn't like senseless horror. But people will cite examples about how crime and torture victims begged God to make it stop and it didn't stop, and they will say that is why they don't pray. And there are horrific stories. But I read that torture book and wondered if maybe some horrors actually are because of a faith or prayer issue, but that the crucial prayers and faith were supposed to be from other people who did not pray or care at important times. And that the evil that is manifest is not because of unanswered prayers but because of unprayed prayers, or because of undone actions that go with faith. That is a crazy thing to say, and it could be even more crazy to say that if it is true, the missing prayers might not be from genuine atheists but from lazy believers. I will still say it, though, because God answers prayer, and why should anyone miss out.

    That was kind of a depressing way to end the book but that is all my thoughts for now. People might think it is stupid to ask God to give a prize package 63 to all the people in countries where they don't even have Doritos or Coke machines, but that is the point, and all the suffering that would make people mad at me is also the point. I am not saying that prayer would fix everything by itself or that a lack of prayer is the root cause of all the evil and suffering. But when you start listing out all the things that you might get if you asked, and listing out all the people who could also get those things, it starts to make sense that maybe at least some people should try to go ahead and pray as much as they can. And of course many people might need to concentrate on other things, like being the people who actually provide some of the health and safety and cheeseburgers and... cash. But even those people probably have some time to ask God for forgiveness, and for some ice cream, and for fifty thousand magical birds to glimmer across a horizon that hides a billion-year harvest for people who did nothing but accept a fraction of the gifts that God loves to give.

    I hope that I have not bothered anyone with any of my attitudes in the book. I just wanted to share some of my prayer ideas, which I thought could help people pray more efficiently and bless more people, and could help some great people go from zero to 45 million in one second. It is true that I have an anxiety disorder behind a lot of my prayer, but I have said before that I think when people break, it is good in at least some ways to try to be broken like a coke machine that gives extra cokes. I think God helped me pray a lot, and to me if writing this book is part of that life, then it could mean that he actually does want to give all this stuff to people, and for more people to be blessed with the asking, too.

The Beatitudes (Matthew 5:1-12)

Now when Jesus saw the crowds, he went up on a mountainside and sat down. His disciples came to him, and he began to teach them.

He said:

"Blessed are the poor in spirit,
for theirs is the kingdom of heaven.

Blessed are those who mourn,
for they will be comforted.

Blessed are the meek,
for they will inherit the earth.

Blessed are those who hunger and thirst for righteousness,
for they will be filled.

Blessed are the merciful,
for they will be shown mercy.

Blessed are the pure in heart,
for they will see God.

Blessed are the peacemakers,
for they will be called children of God.

Blessed are those who are persecuted because of righteousness,
for theirs is the kingdom of heaven.

"Blessed are you when people insult you, persecute you and falsely say all kinds of evil against you because of me. Rejoice and be glad, because great is your reward in heaven, for in the same way they persecuted the prophets who were before you.

Refried Bean is from Greenville, SC.
Refried worked in a bookstore for twelve years
and has an MFA in Writing
from Vermont College of Fine Arts.
Refried has three pet guinea pigs
named Fred, Roger, and Dave.

Made in the USA
Middletown, DE
18 September 2022